Data Response Questions
in Advanced Level Geography

Human Geography

Paul Guinness

Head of Geography, The London Oratory School

HODDER AND STOUGHTON

LONDON   SYDNEY   AUCKLAND   TORONTO

British Library Cataloguing in Publication Data

Guinness, P.
    Data response questions in advanced level geography.
    Human geography
    1. Geography—Examinations, questions, etc.
    I. Title
    910.76   G73

    ISBN 0 340 28326 2

First printed 1983
Third impression 1985

Typeset 11/12pt Plantin (Monophoto) by Macmillan India Ltd,
Bangalore.

Printed in Great Britain for
Hodder and Stoughton Educational,
a division of Hodder and Stoughton Ltd,
Mill Road, Dunton Green, Sevenoaks, Kent TN13 2YD,
by St Edmundsbury Press, Bury St Edmunds, Suffolk.

Contents

Economic Geography

Introduction

In recent years data response questions have become a part of A-level examinations set by an increasing number of examination boards and have usually marked significant changes in syllabus content. The emergence of this style of question at A-level is part of a general move to improve the assessment of a candidate's grasp of the basic concepts upon which modern geography is based. The role of factual recall which tends to dominate the traditional essay answer is deliberately kept to a minimum. Equally, data response questions are designed to test the ability to understand, analyse and apply data and basic techniques in a variety of different forms.

As the style of question differs markedly from the traditional long essay, so the technique required to respond successfully to the format of such structured questions is also different. Practice at tackling data response exercises is thus a vital part of the preparation required for the A-level examination. The aim of this book and its companion *Data Response Questions in Advanced Geography: Physical Geography* is to provide the candidate with a wide range of exercises testing a range of concepts, skills and techniques.

Ideally data response questions should be used over the full duration of the A-level course so that confidence in handling such exercises is gradually acquired. Although the book can also be used as a revision source in the months prior to the examination a longer familiarity with this style of question is advised.

The data response questions set by the examination boards are of two general types; (i) limited data with restricted answer space (e.g. London Board) and (ii) more extensive data where no limitations are placed on the length of the answer (e.g. Joint Matriculation Board). Both varieties of question are contained in this text.

The book falls into three parts covering the elements of population geography, settlement geography and economic geography. Each part is further subdivided into Sections A and B. The questions in Section A are of the limited data – restricted answer type while those in Section B contain more extensive data and require more detailed answers.

Following the format set by the examination boards the exercises in Section A are designed for completion in 15–20 minutes and those in Section B in 35–45 minutes.

For the restricted response questions a guide has been given as to the allocation of marks and the maximum number of lines for the answer for each part of the question, i.e.,

$[5L-8M]$ = 5 lines, 8 marks.

Where a part of a question is further subdivided, $(2 \times [4L-4M])$ = 4 lines, 4 marks for each of the two subdivisions.

In Section B only a suggested mark allocation is provided to retain parity with current examination board policy (i.e., the Joint Matriculation Board). In line with the examination boards the maximum mark for all questions has been set at 25.

The space and mark allocations, finalised after careful testing with A-level students, are offered only as a guide and teachers may wish to amend them where a change in question emphasis is desired.

Due to restrictions of space, where some of the material required for a question can be found in a standard atlas, students are directed to such a source. It is noted that some examination boards are now introducing basic atlases into examinations.

In order to cover as wide a range of topics as possible a basic knowledge of socio-economic conditions in the United Kingdom has been assumed in a small number of questions.

Acknowledgements

The author and the publishers would like to thank the following for permission to reproduce copyright material in this book: Question 2 – The Longman Group Ltd; Questions 4 and 18 – *World Bank Atlas*; Question 6 – Edward Arnold (Publishers) Ltd for a table from *Population analysis and models* by L. Henry; Question 9 – *Financial Times*; Questions 10, 20, 24, 48 and 88 – data from *World Population Trends and Policies: 1979 Monitoring Report*, United Nations publication, Sales No. 79, XIII, 4; Question 77 – statistics from UN *Monthly Bulletin of Statistics*, copyright, United Nations (1981), reproduced by permission; Question 13 – OECD, Paris for a table from *Continuous Reporting System on Migration*; material in questions 19, 23, 25, 27, 54, 75, 76, 78, 80, 87 and 90 is reproduced with the permission of the Controller of Her Majesty's Stationery Office, sources: Questions 19, 27 and 54 – Office of Population Censuses and Surveys; Questions 23, 76 and 80 – *Regional Trends*, 1981; Question 25 – *Population Trends 25*, Autumn 1981 (HMSO, 1981) and *International Migration 1979* Series MN No. 6 (HMSO, 1981); Question 75 – *Transport Statistics*; Question 78 – *Statistical News* (54) August 1981; Question 87 – Central Statistical Office; Question 90 – Department of Trade; Question 21 – *Daily Express*; Question 26 – *The Guardian*; Question 32 – Gustav Fischer Verlag for a diagram from *The Economics of Location* by A. Losch; Question 37 – Routledge and Kegan Paul Ltd for a diagram from *An Approach to Urban Sociology* by Peter Mann; Questions 41 and 45 – Oxford University Press for maps from *An Introduction to Social Geography* by E. Jones and J. Eyles © Oxford University Press 1977 and from *A Social Atlas of London* by Shepherd, Westaway and Lee © Oxford University Press 1974; Question 43 – from Jean Gottmann, *Megalopolis: The Urbanized Northeastern Seaboard of the United States*, copyright 1961 by the Twentieth Century Fund, used with permission; Question 44 – from 'The Internal Structure of African Cities' by J. W. Sommer in *Contemporary Africa: Geography and Change*, edited by C. G. Knight and James L. Newman, © 1976, p. 311, reprinted by permission of Prentice-Hall, Inc., Englewood Cliffs, N. J.; Question 50 – *The Economist*; Question 66 – V. H. Winston and Sons for material from *Nonmetropolitan Industrialization* by R. E. Lonsdale and H. L. Seyler; Question 77 – Thomas Nelson and Sons Ltd for a diagram from *Man and His World* by J. Dawson and D. Thomas; Question 81 – a map reproduced by permission of the publishers of *ABC Air Travel Atlas*; Question 84 – U.K. Offshore Operators Association Limited; Question 89 – European Brazilian Bank Ltd.

Population Geography – Section A

1

(a) Describe the differences between the three models. *(8L–7M)*

(b) Suggest possible reasons for the absence of a period of rapid growth in model B. *(6L–6M)*

(c) Account for the rise in the birth rate in model C. *(6L–6M)*

(d) How applicable are these models to the less developed world? *(6L–6M)*

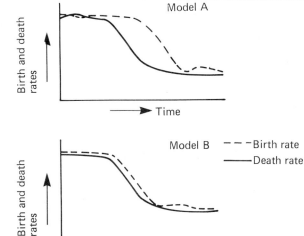

Models of demographic transition

2

'The demographic explosion is taking place in countries where the economy is underdeveloped and where the social mechanism limiting fertility is absent.' (Leszek Kosinski)

(a) What are the approximate growth rate limits in the less developed world? *(2L–3M)*

(b) Which developments led to 'the demographic explosion'? *(6L–6M)*

(c) How far are economic conditions affected by demographic trends? *(9L–8M)*

(d) What is 'the social mechanism limiting fertility'? *(9L–8M)*

3

(a) Insert the data missing from the table. *(4M)*

(b) In terms of the model of demographic transition, in which stage might England and Wales be placed in the following years (i) 1751 (ii) 1851 (iii) 1951? *(3 × [1L–1M])*

(c) Account for the decline in the death rate over the period. *(10L–9M)*

(d) Why did the decline in birth rate follow at a much later date? *(10L–9M)*

Population statistics: England and Wales

Year	Birth rate	Death rate	Natural increase
1751	35.0	30.0	5.0
1801	34.0	23.0	11.0
1851	33.9	22.7	11.2
1901	26.7	15.1	11.6
1951	15.9	11.6	4.3
1980	13.3	11.8	1.5

4

(a) What percentage of world population has a growth rate of more than 2% per annum?

(*1L–4M*)

(b) Define the following terms: (i) Average G.N.P. per capita, (ii) Population growth rate.

(*2 × [3L–3M]*)

(c) Name two countries which have growth rates of (i) less than 1%, (ii) more than 3%.

(*2 × [1L–2M]*)

(d) Examine the relationship between population growth rate and average G.N.P. per capita.

(*11L–11M*)

Population (mid-1978), by 1970–78 growth rate levels

Growth	Number of countries	Population mid-1978 (millions)	GNP 1978 (U.S. $ 000 millions)	Average GNP per capita 1978 (U.S. $)
Less than 1.0%	35	912	5853	6419
1.0% to less than 2.0%	40	1420	1824	1284
2.0% to less than 2.5%	27	949	283	298
2.5% to less than 3.0%	41	663	486	733
3.0% and over	35	216	347	1608

5

(a) In which time period was the fastest rate of growth experienced by (i) country A, (ii) country B?

(*2 × [1L–2M]*)

(b) By what percentage did the population grow between 1700 and 1975 in (i) country A, (ii) country B?

(*2 × [1L–2M]*)

(c) Why is the change in country B irregular compared to the developed world as a whole?

(*8L–8M*)

(d) Suggest possible reasons for the irregularities shown.

(*10L–9M*)

Time	Country A	Country B
1700	2.0 million	2.5 million
1750	2.0 "	3.0 "
1800	2.0 "	5.25 "
1850	3.0 %	6.5 "
1900	5.25 "	4.5 "
1950	10.0 "	4.25 "
1980	14.1 "	4.9 "

6

(a) How many of the French population were 20 years old on the 1st January 1968? (*1L–4M*)

(b) Account for the deficits at the points marked A and B. (*6L–6M*)

(c) Give two reasons to explain the very low number of males aged 80 years and over.

(*6L–8M*)

(d) What can be deduced from the pyramid concerning trends in the birth rate between 1947 and 1967? (*8L–7M*)

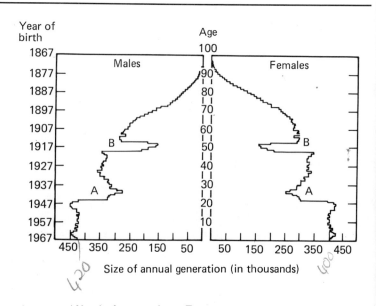

Age pyramid by single years of age: France 1st January 1968

7

(a) What percentage of the population is (i) over 65?
(ii) under 15? $(2 \times [1L-2M])$

(b) Suggest a possible location for this country.
                                                $(1L-1M)$

(c) Analyse the graph in terms of the following:
(i) birth rate (ii) death rate (iii) rate of natural
increase (iv) sex ratio (v) dependency ratio.
                                                $(5 \times [4L-4M])$

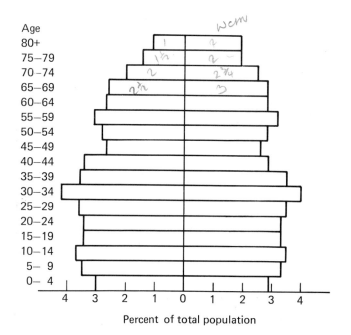

A population pyramid, 1979

8

(a) The pyramids show the age/sex structure of the
United States and Mexico. Which country's
population is illustrated by (i) Pyramid A,
(ii) Pyramid B? $(2L-2M)$

(b) In which stage of demographic transition is
(i) Pyramid A, (ii) Pyramid B? $(2L-4M)$

(c) Assess and explain the contrasting percentages
of population under 15 and over 65 years in the
two countries. $(10L-10M)$

(d) What is the socio-economic impact of large
numbers in these age groups? $(10L-9M)$

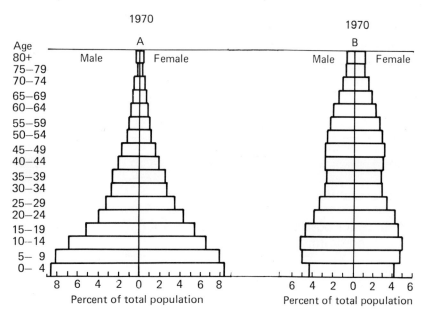

9

(a) Define (i) birth rate, (ii) fertility rate, (iii) replacement level. *(3 × [3L–2M])*

(b) Account for the general decline in fertility shown in the graph. *(10L–12M)*

(c) Suggest possible reasons for the contrasting fertility levels of Poland and West Germany. *(6L–7M)*

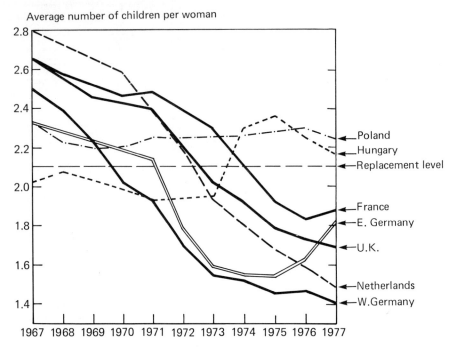

The decline in European fertility

IO

(a) Define infant mortality rate. *(3L–4M)*

(b) Suggest reasons for the variations in infant mortality shown in the table. *(12L–13M)*

(c) How far are variations in infant mortality linked to differences in crude death rate? *(8L–8M)*

Infant mortality rates 1975

Yemen	210	Kuwait	43
Bolivia	162	Jamaica	27
Bangladesh	153	Singapore	14

II

With reference to a long-term migration between two countries:

(a) Assess the importance of major positive and negative factors at origin and destination. *(10L–12M)*

(b) How have the intervening obstacles changed over time? *(11L–13M)*

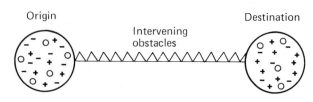

+ Positive factors   − Negative factors

o Factors perceived as unimportant to the individual

A basic migration model

12

(a) Complete the table by providing an example for each type of migration. *(5M)*

(b) Explain the circumstances of a forced migration occurring in recent years (after 1970). *(10L–10M)*

(c) What are the likely effects of a mass migration on the age structure of (i) the emigrant country, (ii) the immigrant country? *(2 × [6L–5M])*

W. Petersen's migration typology (1958)

Type	Example
1. Primitive	
2. Impelled	
3. Forced	
4. Free	
5. Mass	

13

(a) In rank order which three countries supply the greatest number of foreign workers to countries in northern and western Europe? *(2L–6M)*

(b) How important is distance to such movements? *(6L–6M)*

(c) Identify the other important factors governing the number of foreign workers in the nations listed. *(12L–13M)*

Estimated number of foreign workers, Northern and Western Europe, 1976

Country of origin	Austria	Belgium	France	Germany Federal Republic of	Luxem-bourg	Nether-lands	Sweden	Switzer-land	United Kingdom
Total	171 700	316 800	1 584 300	1 937 100	46 800	180 500	235 500	516 040	866 000
Algeria	. . .	3500	331 100	1400	. . .	. . .	200	. . .	500
Austria	. . .	1000	. . .	76 000	. . .	. . .	3100	20 413	3000
Finland	. . .	—	—	—	. . .	. . .	105 000	. . .	1000
Greece	. . .	10 000	. . .	178 800	. . .	2200	9000	5165	10 500
Italy	1700	96 000	199 200	276 400	10 700	10 100	3000	261 566	56 500
Morocco	. . .	28 000	152 300	15 600	. . .	29 100	500	. . .	500
Portugal	. . .	6000	360 700	63 600	12 500	5000	1100	4144	3000
Spain	200	30 000	204 000	111 000	1900	16 000	1900	68 894	24 000
Tunisia	. . .	2000	73 000	12 000	. . .	1000	300	. . .	—
Turkey	24 600	16 000	31 200	527 500	. . .	38 200	3800	15 168	4500
Yugoslavia	120 500	3000	42 200	390 100	600	9500	27 000	24 110	8500
Others	24 700	121 300	190 600	296 100	21 100	70 000	80 600	116 560	753 500

14

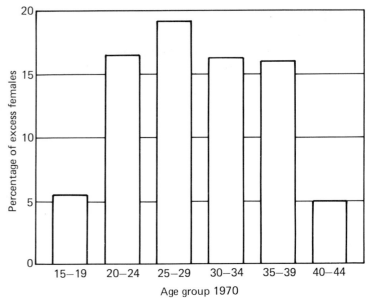

Age group 1970

(a) Summarise the information shown on the graph. *(8L–6M)*

(b) Suggest possible reasons for such a population imbalance. *(6L–8M)*

(c) Under what circumstances might a balanced sex-ratio eventually be achieved? *(10L–11M)*

15

(a) What is meant by (i) Arithmetical progression? (ii) Geometrical progress? *(2 × [3L–3M])*

(b) List three possible 'limiting factors' which might check population growth. *(3 × [1L–1M])*

(c) Describe four ways in which food production has increased beyond the levels thought possible by Malthus. *(4 × [4L–4M])*

Malthus's relationship between food supply and population

Year	0	20	40	60	80	100	Progression
Units food supply	1	2	3	4	5	6	Arithmetical
Units population	1	2	4	8	16	32	Geometrical

16

(a) Why is Asia generally considered the most 'overpopulated' continent? *(8L–8M)*

(b) What is meant by (i) Underpopulation? (ii) Optimum population? (iii) Maximum population? *(3 × [3L–3M])*

(c) Give four indicators of population pressure in the developed world. *(4 × [2L–2M])*

Population density per square kilometre

Africa	11	Asia	68
North America	10	Europe	91
Latin America	12	Oceania	2

17

(a) Explain the terms (i) Economic optimum, (ii) Power optimum. $(2 \times [5L-5M])$

(b) How might socio-economic conditions differ between two countries, one pursuing the power optimum and the other the economic optimum as a matter of policy? $(14L-15M)$

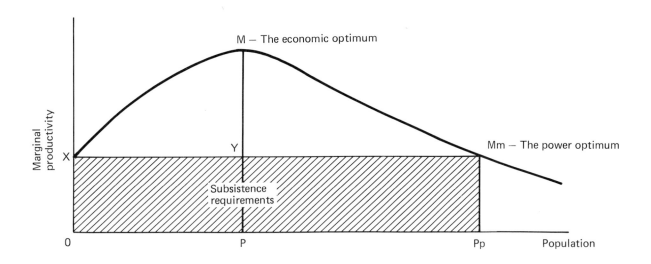

18

Countries with per capita incomes of—

Less than $300: Afghanistan, Bangladesh, Benin, Bhutan, Burma, Burundi, Cape Verde, Central African Republic, Chad, China, Comoros, Cuba, Ethiopia, The Gambia, Guinea, Guinea-Bissau, Haiti, India, Madagascar, Malawi, Maldives, Mali, Mauritania, Mozambique, Nepal, Niger, Pakistan, Rwanda, Sierra Leone, Somalia, Sri Lanka, Tanzania, Uganda, Upper Volta, Western Samoa, Zaire.

$7,000 and over: American Samoa, Australia, Austria, Belgium, Bermuda, Brunei, Canada, Denmark, Faeroe Islands, Finland, France, Federal Republic of Germany, Greenland, Iceland, Japan, Kuwait, Libya, Luxembourg, The Netherlands, Norway, Qatar, Sweden, Switzerland, United Arab Emirates, United States.

(a) Attempt to divide the countries with per capita incomes of $7000 and over into broad categories to explain the reasons for their affluence. $(10L-10M)$

(b) To what extent is per capita income a useful indicator of a country's economic strength? $(6L-5M)$

(c) Describe the demographic trends which are generally common to the countries with per capita incomes of less than $300. $(12L-10M)$

19

(a) Explain the dominant factors behind the declining population of Greater London and the Metropolitan districts. *(10L–10M)*

(b) Isolate the reasons for the increasing rate of population growth in the remoter rural areas. *(8L–8M)*

(c) Briefly explain the lower national rate of population growth 1971–81 compared to the 1961–71 period. *(9L–7M)*

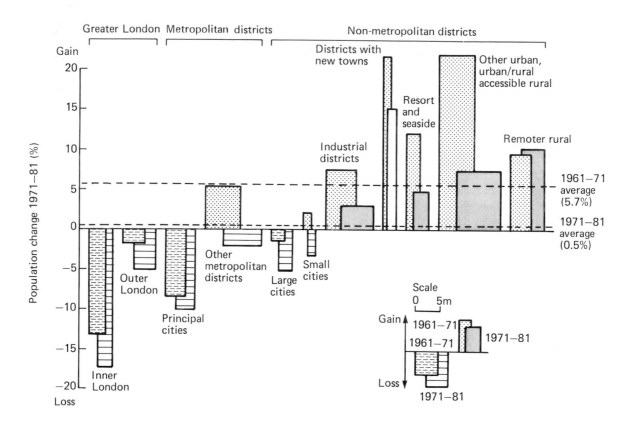

Percentage population change, 1971–81 and 1961–71, by type of district

20

(a) Briefly describe the basic differences between the more developed countries and the less developed countries in terms of the percentage of school enrolled children for the two age ranges. *(8L–6M)*

(b) Discuss reasons for the varying female participation rate in education for the different regions. *(8L–8M)*

(c) Is there a significant relationship between (i) education and fertility levels in the less developed world and (ii) education and economic development? *(10L–11M)*

Proportion of population school enrolled for age groups 6–11 and 12–17

| | | Age group 6–11 | | Age group 12–17 | |
| | | Proportion enrolled (%) | | Proportion enrolled (%) | |
	Year	Total	Females	Total	Females
More developed countries	1960	91.3	91.3	72.6	71.2
	1975	93.9	93.9	84.3	84.9
Less developed countries	1960	46.3	36.6	21.5	14.7
	1975	61.6	53.3	35.2	28.1
Africa	1960	32.9	24.9	17.3	11.4
	1975	51.1	43.3	31.2	23.5
Latin America	1960	58.5	58.0	36.2	33.5
	1975	77.9	78.2	56.5	54.5
South Asia	1960	47.6	35.0	19.4	11.5
	1975	60.6	49.8	30.6	22.5

21

NOW FRANCE LAUNCHES AN £11 BILLION CAMPAIGN TO BOOST PRODUCTIVITY BY JACK GEE in Paris

GENERAL DE GAULLE must be turning in his grave.

His fellow countrymen – and particularly the women – don't seem to care a hoot about his target to produce 100 million citizens by the turn of the century.

A high birth rate, the General told them almost 20 years ago, was the only guarantee for the French to maintain their status as a major power.

Not only against their enemies. But also against their allies – including Britain. Today President Giscard d'Estaing faces the threat that, far from doubling their numbers, the French will find their population shrinking in the relatively near future.

Michel Debré, the veteran Gaullist politician who hopes to stand against Giscard for president next year says: "Babies do not vote. But a Republic which failed to build its own future is no longer a Republic."

DANGER

To ward off this danger Giscard is offering lavish new inducements to mothers to produce more children. The cost of France's family-boosting programme will soon exceed £11 Billion the French Exchequer's entire revenue from Income Tax

The problem is simple. Two-child families nearly keep the population level by replacing the parents.

It is only the third child which represents an extra citizen for the future.

But in France the average couple do not even produce two offspring. Only 1.8.

Giscard has decided to play for high stakes in encouraging parents to have three children. In this game of

Happy Families his cards, which he hopes will turn out trumps, include:

● Payment at the birth of baby no. 3 of a lump sum of £1,064. The existing maternity grant of £462, paid over two years, will thus be more than doubled.

● A guaranteed minimum family income of £447 a month. This will be provided by generous allowances to supplement wages.

● A promise that this purchasing power of a three-child family will increase by at least three per cent a year – again thanks to family allowances.

● Maternity leave will be increased to six months on full pay. Until now mothers have got four months off.

● To enable these prolific and patriotic households to live in comfort, 100 per cent mortgages will be available. And they will get priority to rent three-bedroom council flats.

● Full tax benefits for parents will continue until the youngest child of the trio is 18 years-old – even if the elder brothers and sisters are already wage earners.

● The 30 per cent fare reduction, already available on public transport, will now apply to the entire family until the last child reaches his majority.

● A pension scheme for mothers is to be introduced. The French government now recognises that being a mum is just as strenuous a career as that of a male bread-winner.

● "Keep off the grass" notices are being removed from public parks and squares. Somebody must have told Giscard that space for children to play is as important as cash benefits.

● Non-working mothers of big families will get the same access to day nurseries, canteens and holiday camps as women in full-time jobs.

DECLINE

● The Government will do its best to persuade employers to let mothers work part-time or take a day off on Wednesday, which is a weekly school holiday in France.

Many of these new advantages will take effect almost immediately. Others will be introduced in France's next budget – well before April 1981, when Giscard is banking on a second seven-year spell at the Elysee Palace. But this Happy Families deal is much more than a piece of smart electioneering.

The statisticians are making gloomy predictions about a decline in France's population unless urgent action is taken. Giscard wants to go down in history as the man who helped to reverse this trend.

One baby is best Chinese are told

COUPLES who have more than one child in Pill-conscious China these days must pay for their sins.

As soon as the second baby is born, they have to return in full the family allowance given for the first.

Since the £1.35 allowance is paid every month for 10 years, returning it is a severe hardship.

This is just one of the ways the Peking authorities are making the point that one is best.

A single child is granted priority entry to nurseries and hospitals.

Education benefits go all the way to universities.

In rural districts, privileges for the single-child farming families include enlarged private land plots and increased grain rations.

The Government's aim is to cut the growth rate to zero by the year 2000.

At the moment it is running at 1.17 per cent—officially described as "unacceptable."

The latest Government estimates of population say that there are nearly 971 million people on the mainland.

But this is thought to be optimistically low. American experts reckon that the 1,000 million mark was passed several years ago.

The two extracts from newspaper reports describe government attempts to influence the rate of population growth.

(a) Suggest why some governments are anxious to increase their rate of population growth while most countries adopt a non-interventionist or reverse policy. (7M)

(b) Compare the ways in which the French and Chinese governments are attempting to influence population trends in their respective countries. (6M)

(c) What role does a high rate of population growth play in the so called 'vicious circle of poverty'. (5M)

(d) Describe how one named less developed country (other than China) has attempted to lower its fertility rate. How successful has the policy been? (7M)

22

(a) Assess the importance of international migration to the change in total population. *(5M)*

(b) In 1951 the total population was 2.961 million. If net emigration had been zero in the next decade, what would the total population have been in 1961? *(8M)*

(c) How far have total population trends varied between the four provinces? *(4M)*

(d) Suggest possible reasons for the general increase in the marriage rate from 1881 to 1979. *(4M)*

(e) How applicable are the trends shown by the data to the developed world in general? *(4M)*

Population (thousands)

Census figures	Ireland Total	Males	Females	Leinster Total	Munster	Connaught	Ulster (part)
1841	6529	3223	3306	1974	2396	1419	740
1861	4402	2169	2233	1458	1513	913	518
1881	3870	1912	1958	1279	1331	822	438
1901	3222	1610	1612	1153	1076	647	346
1926	2971	1507	1465	1149	970	553	300
1946	2955	1495	1460	1281	917	493	264
1951	2961	1507	1454	1337	899	472	253
1956	2898	1463	1435	1339	877	446	236
1961	2818	1416	1402	1332	849	419	218
1966	2884	1449	1435	1414	859	402	208
1971	2978	1496	1482	1498	882	391	207
1979	3364	1692	1672	1742	979	418	226

Marriage, Birth, Death and Emigration Rates (per thousand average population per annum)

Period	Marriage rate	Birth rate	Death rate	Natural increase (births-deaths)	Change in population	Estimated net emigration
1881–1891	4.0	22.8	17.4	5.3	−10.9	16.3
1901–1911	4.8	22.4	16.8	5.6	−2.6	8.2
1926–1936	4.6	19.6	14.2	5.5	−0.1	5.6
1946–1951	5.5	22.2	13.6	8.6	+0.4	8.2
1951–1956	5.4	21.3	12.2	9.2	−4.3	13.4
1956–1961	5.4	21.2	11.9	9.2	−5.6	14.8
1961–1966	5.7	21.9	11.7	10.3	+4.6	5.7
1966–1971	6.5	21.3	11.2	10.1	+6.4	3.7
1971–1979	6.8	21.6	10.5	11.1	+15.4	−4.3

23

(a) Define (i) Infant mortality rate, (ii) Crude death rate. *(2M)*

(b) Using Spearman's Rank Correlation Coefficient

$$\left(R = 1 - \frac{6 \times \sum d^2}{(n^3 - n)}\right)$$

calculate the relationship between infant mortality rates and crude death rates for the eleven regions in 1979. Comment on your results. *(9M)*

(c) Why did the death rate rise in most regions between 1961 and 1979 while the infant mortality rate universally declined? *(6M)*

(d) Identify two factors which could cause the death rate in the U.K. to decline in the future. *(4M)*

(e) Suggest possible reasons for regional variations in infant mortality rates. *(4M)*

	Infant mortality rate					Crude death rate				
	1961	1966	1971	1978	1979	1961	1966	1971	1978	1979
United Kingdom	22.1	19.6	17.9	13.3	12.9	12.0	11.8	11.6	12.0	12.1
North	23.2	21.1	18.6	13.9	13.3	11.9	12.3	12.0	12.5	12.7
Yorkshire and Humberside	23.9	22.3	19.9	13.3	13.9	12.5	12.3	12.1	12.3	12.5
East Midlands	19.8	19.3	18.2	13.4	12.4	11.2	11.4	11.1	11.5	11.6
East Anglia	18.2	17.5	15.2	10.8	12.6	11.6	11.2	11.2	11.6	11.2
South East	19.5	16.9	15.9	12.8	11.9	11.5	11.3	11.2	11.4	11.5
South West	18.5	16.8	16.0	12.4	12.5	12.4	12.4	12.4	12.6	12.9
West Midlands	22.1	19.5	17.7	13.7	13.8	10.9	10.8	10.4	10.9	11.2
North West	25.0	21.6	19.7	13.7	13.5	13.3	12.8	12.5	12.7	12.9
England	21.3	18.9	17.5	13.1	12.8	11.9	11.7	11.5	11.8	12.0
Wales	24.0	20.3	18.4	13.2	12.4	12.8	12.9	12.8	13.0	13.0
Scotland	25.8	23.2	19.9	12.9	12.8	12.3	12.2	11.8	12.6	12.7
Northern Ireland	27.5	25.6	22.7	15.9	14.8	11.3	11.1	10.6	10.5	10.9

24

(a) (i) Plot the birth rate against the rate of natural increase for the eight world regions listed in the table. *(6M)*

   (ii) What does the graph show about the relationship between the two variables? *(2M)*

(b) The transition stage of the model of demographic transition can be subdivided into early, middle and late transition. Place each of the four regions in the less developed world into one of these subdivisions. *(4M)*

(c) Explain the differences in birth rate between these four regions. *(7M)*

(d) Account for variations in the death rate between the eight regions. *(6M)*

Region	Population 1978 (M)	Average Birth Rate 1975–80	Average Death Rate 1975–80
Less developed world	2940	33.6	12.0
Africa	406	46.0	17.1
Latin America	323	35.4	8.4
East Asia	1063	22.2[1]	8.8[1]
South Asia	1255	38.9	14.0
More Developed World	1093	15.6	9.4
North America	236	15.3	9.0
Europe	474	14.5	10.6
U.S.S.R	254	18.3	8.9
Oceania	21	16.8[2]	7.9[2]

[1] Excluding Japan
[2] Australia and N. Zealand only.

25

(a) How true is it that U.K. international migration is selective in terms of age? (5M)

(b) (i) Identify the focal points of immigration into the United Kingdom (ii) What are the main factors influencing the regional destination of immigrants? (6M)

(c) Attempt to explain why the U.K. has a positive migration balance with the New Commonwealth and Pakistan but a negative balance with most of the Old Commonwealth and the U.S. (7M)

(d) For one country examine the socio-economic effects of a sustained period of net immigration. (7M)

U.K. International Migration by Age (Thousands)

Immigrants	Under 15 years	15–24	25–44	45 +	All ages
1976	32.4	64.0	77.1	17.8	191.3
1977	29.0	55.2	64.8	13.5	162.6
1978	38.0	57.9	71.7	19.4	187.0
1979	35.5	64.2	78.0	17.3	194.8
Emigrants					
1976	40.2	51.7	97.2	21.2	210.4
1977	30.7	53.8	101.5	22.7	208.7
1978	28.6	54.0	91.1	18.7	192.4
1979	29.5	51.1	90.3	17.7	188.6

Destination of Immigrants by Region (Thousands)

Year	Wales	Scotland	N. Ireland	North	North West	Yorkshire & Humberside	West Midlands	East Midlands	East Anglia	South East	South West
1976	2.9	12.1	0.6	5.3	15.0	12.9	17.0	6.9	3.8	102.1	12.9
1977	4.2	12.5	0.7	4.1	15.8	11.1	9.7	6.1	3.2	87.0	8.3
1978	7.1	9.4	1.6	4.0	15.2	11.0	18.3	9.8	6.2	93.4	11.1
1979	4.8	12.3	1.5	5.0	14.7	12.5	16.2	6.3	5.6	101.2	14.7

U. K. Immigration and Emigration in 1979 (Thousands)

Immigrants		Emigrants 1979	
All countries	194.8	*All countries*	188.6
Commonwealth countries	91.9	*Commonwealth countries*	76.2
Australia	16.1	Australia	23.4
Canada	6.0	Canada	19.0
New Zealand	8.6	New Zealand	7.8
African Commonwealth	17.1	African Commonwealth	9.1
Bangladesh, India, Sri Lanka	18.9	Bangladesh, India, Sri Lanka	4.0
West Indies	5.3	West Indies	2.9
Other Commonwealth	20.0	Other Commonwealth	10.0
Foreign countries	102.9	*Foreign countries*	112.4
European Community	22.6	European Community	28.8
Remainder of Europe	11.4	Remainder of Europe	12.2
United States of America	13.4	United States of America	26.3
Remainder of America	2.8	Remainder of America	4.2
Republic of South Africa	11.1	Republic of South Africa	6.1
Pakistan	14.4	Pakistan	1.7
Middle East	14.3	Middle East	23.3
Other Foreign	12.8	Other Foreign	9.8

Are old people a problem with a capital P or rather a valuable natural resource?

There are now about twice as many over-60s as there were in 1950, then put at 214 million. By 2025, when today's teenagers will be joining the over-60s, there will be an estimated 1.12 billion.

This is part of the population explosion, the part that does not get the same attention as the birth rate. We tend to think first of the children, and quite understandably so. In 1975 the under-15s accounted for 41 per cent of the population in the developing countries where the over-60s numbered only 6 per cent. But in these countries 50 years on it is forecast the proportion of under-15s will have fallen to 26 per cent and the over-60 survivors will have climbed to 12 per cent.

This shift in the balance of the world's population is one of those dramatic changes going on all around us in this extraordinary century. It ought to count as big news but in practice is often pushed aside as just another heap of boring statistics. Understandably so, but I will make just one more statistical point.

This shift has gone furthest and is still moving fastest in the developed countries of Europe, North America and the Pacific. Here the expectation of life — how long you can expect to live — has moved up from the middle 50s 50 years ago to around 70 to 75 now. These averages imply that many more people will be living well beyond 75. In Europe the percentage of the population over 60 has increased by half in the past 30 years, and by the year 2025 is expected to reach 25 per cent, double what it was in 1950.

Current trends suggest that average life expectancy will not go much above 75, but with a low birth rate there will be in the population of the future a relatively smaller proportion of young people.

(a) Why do the elderly form a much higher percentage of population in the developed world compared to the less developed world? *(4M)*

(b) To what extent will this distinction be maintained in the next 50 years? *(4M)*

(c) In which ways might an increasingly elderly population put pressure on a country's resources? *(6M)*

(d) Conversely, how might the elderly be regarded as a 'valuable natural resource'? *(6M)*

(e) What influence might the trends described in the extract have on population policies in the developed world? *(5M)*

27

(a) What is the Standardized Fertility Ratio? *(3M)*

(b) Why is the fertility rate generally regarded as a more important demographic indicator than the crude birth rate? *(4M)*

(c) For the country as a whole explain fertility variations between the various age groups. *(6M)*

(d) Suggest reasons for the differences recorded in the regions. *(6M)*

(e) To what extent and why did the level of fertility change in 1979 compared to the previous year? *(6M)*

Fertility rates in the United Kingdom

| | Live births per 1,000 women in age groups: | | | | | | | SFR[3] (GB = 100) |
	15–44[1]	15–19[2]	20–24	25–29	30–34	35–39	40–44	
1978								
Great Britain	61	30	108	124	64	20	4	100.0
North	62	36	121	123	56	16	3	101.6
Yorkshire and Humberside	61	33	119	121	56	17	5	99.0
East Midlands	61	32	109	125	60	17	4	101.4
East Anglia	60	25	108	125	62	16	3	98.5
South East	61	25	99	127	72	22	4	101.0
South West	57	25	100	119	61	18	4	90.8
West Midlands	62	33	114	121	62	21	5	101.8
North West	61	34	113	123	61	20	5	100.5
England	61	30	107	124	64	20	4	99.8
Wales	61	35	116	120	57	18	4	99.0
Scotland	61	33	109	124	62	18	4	101.7
Northern Ireland[4]	85	31	133	176	110	51	13	139.8
1979								
Great Britain	64	31	112	133	70	21	4	100.0
North	67	38	128	136	64	17	3	103.8
Yorkshire and Humberside	64	35	123	129	62	18	4	98.4
East Midlands	64	33	113	132	65	19	4	100.5
East Anglia	63	26	110	132	70	20	4	98.3
South East	64	26	103	136	78	24	5	100.5
South West	60	25	102	127	67	19	3	90.0
West Midlands	65	35	118	133	66	22	5	101.8
North West	65	36	119	132	67	22	5	101.3
England	64	30	112	133	70	22	4	99.7
Wales	65	36	121	130	65	21	4	100.3
Scotland[4]	64	33	112	133	67	21	4	101.8
Northern Ireland	..	..	..	..	..	..	..	..

(1) Births to mothers aged under 15 and 45 and over have been included in the aggregate 15–44
(2) Births to mothers aged under 15 have been included in the age group 15–19
(3) SFR = Standardized Fertility Ratio
(4) Provisional

Settlement Geography – Section A

28

(a) Suggest five possible criteria for the zones of influence shown (excluding questionnaire analysis). (5M)

(b) Why is there a marked difference between the zones? (7L–7M)

(c) Why would it be important for a large retail firm to assess the zone of influence before a location decision is made? (7L–7M)

(d) How could questionaire analysis be used to determine the zone of influence of a city? (6L–6M)

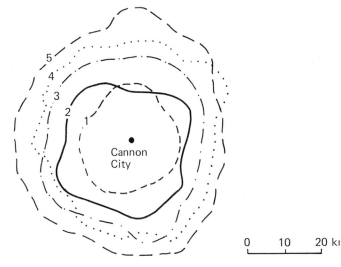

Cannon City – zones of influence

29

(a) What is meant by the urban zone of influence? (5L–5M)

(b) List four methods by which the zone of influence can be deliminated. (4 × [2L–2M])

(c) Suggest possible reasons for the occurrence of distorted and truncated zones. (10L–12M)

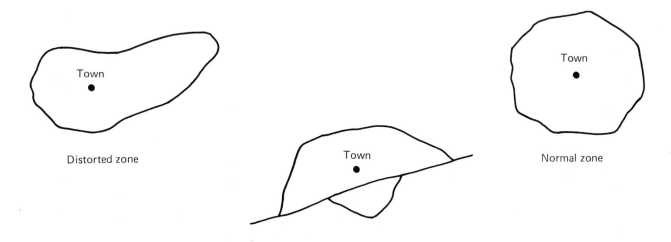

Distorted zone

Truncated zone

Normal zone

Urban zone of influence

30

The Breaking Point Theory

$$d_{jk} = \frac{d_{ij}}{1 + \sqrt{P_i/P_j}}$$

Where d_{jk} is the distance of j (smaller town) from the breaking point k

d_{ij} is the distance between towns i and j

P_i is the population of town i

P_j is the population of j

(a) Calculate the breaking point between the two towns. *(3L–7M)*

(b) Outline the theoretical basis of the theory. *(6L–6M)*

(c) Identify three factors which could result in a breaking point different from the answer above. *(3 × [4L–4M])*

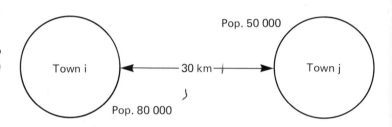

Pop. 50 000

Town i ←————— 30 km —|—→ Town j

Pop. 80 000

31

(a) According to Christaller, what is the K-value of this settlement pattern? *(1L–5M)*

K = 3.

(b) Account for the hexagonal shape of the market areas. *(6L–6M)*

(c) Comment on the relationship between the number and size of settlements. *(7L–7M)*

(d) What did Christaller mean by an 'isotropic surface'? *(8L–7M)*

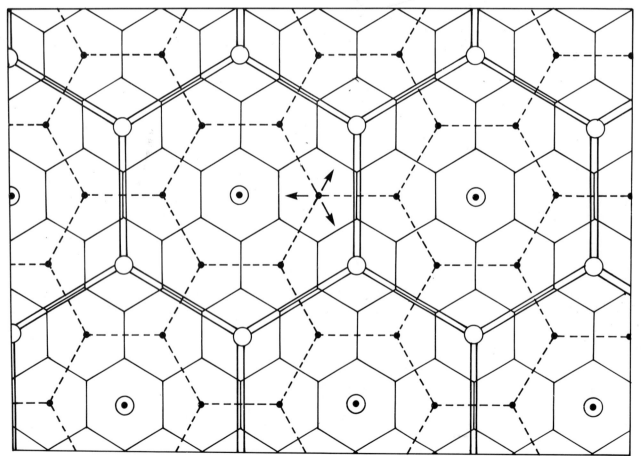

Christaller's Central Place Model

32

(a) Account for the hexagonal shaped market areas.

(5L–5M)

(b) How does the Loschian landscape differ from Christaller's K-3 network?

(8L–8M)

(c) Explain the terms (i) Economic landscape, (ii) City rich sector and (iii) City poor sector.

(3 × [4L–4M])

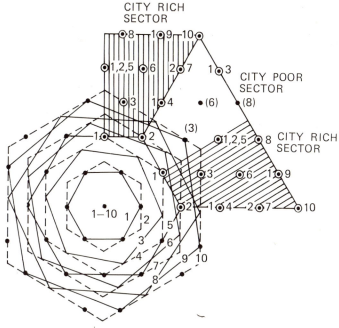

- • Original settlements
- ⊙ Centres of market areas of sizes indicated by figures Alternative regional centres are in parentheses

The ten smallest possible market areas

33

(a) Which term could be used to describe the settlement pattern in (i) Fig. A, (ii) Fig. B and (iii) Fig. C?

(3 × [1L–2M])

(b) Outline the human and physical factors which might result in; (i) Fig. A, (ii) Fig. B and (iii) Fig. C.

(3 × [6L–5M])

(c) Describe a statistical technique that can be used to assess the pattern of distribution.

(5L–4M)

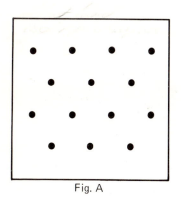

Fig. A

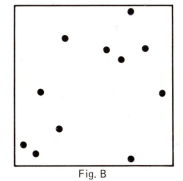

Fig. B

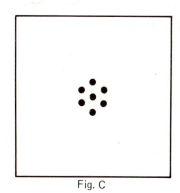

Fig. C

34

(a) On a tracing of the graph insert the regression line that would result if there were a perfect rank-size relationship. (5M)

(b) Explain why the United Kingdom has a primate pattern. (10L–10M)

(c) Under what economic circumstances is a regular rank-size relationship more likely than a primate pattern? (10L–10M)

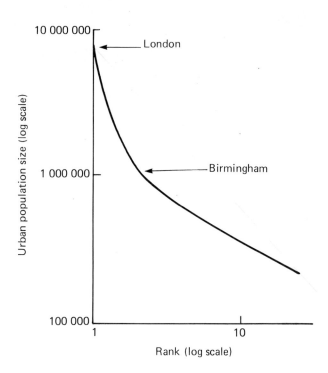

United Kingdom: urban rank size relationship

35

(a) (i) Which dominant factor is used to explain the concentric zonation of land use? (1L–3M)

   (ii) What is the usual name given to zone one? (1L–2M)

(b) Explain the concepts of invasion and succession. (8L–7M)

(c) Comment on three points on which the model has been criticised. (3 × [4L–3M])

(d) Name two later models which attempted to improve upon the concentric zone model. (2L–4M)

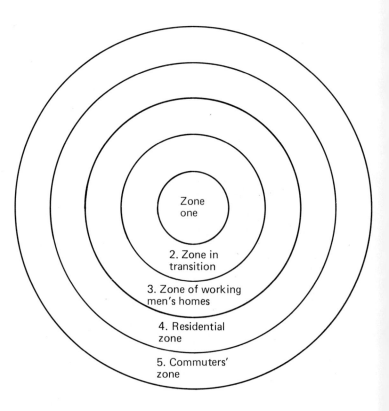

Concentric zone model of urban structure

36

(a) Identify the two models of urban structure shown in Figs. A and B. *(2L–4M)*

(b) In Fig. A why are the land use zones arranged in segments? *(6L–6M)*

(c) In Fig. B comment on the position of the following:
(i) Wholesale light manufacturing, (ii) Outlying business district and (iii) Heavy manufacturing.
(3 × [6L–5M])

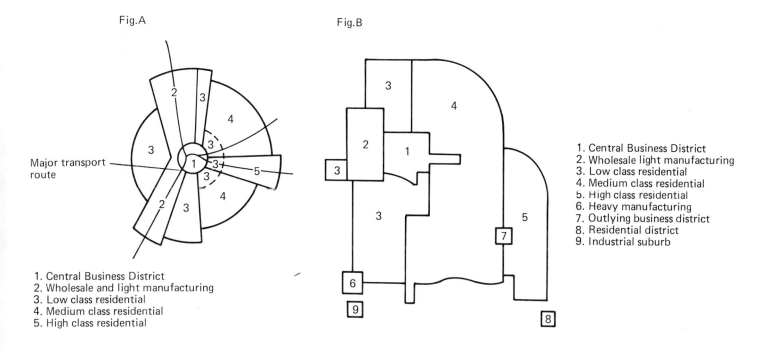

Fig.A

Major transport route

1. Central Business District
2. Wholesale and light manufacturing
3. Low class residential
4. Medium class residential
5. High class residential

Fig.B

1. Central Business District
2. Wholesale light manufacturing
3. Low class residential
4. Medium class residential
5. High class residential
6. Heavy manufacturing
7. Outlying business district
8. Residential district
9. Industrial suburb

37

(a) The diagram attempts to relate which two urban land use theories to British cities? *(2L–4M)*

(b) Give two reasons for the location of the Industrial zone. *(6L–6M)*

(c) Which factors might contribute to the location of the middle class sector? *(6L–6M)*

(d) How far is the model an improvement on the theories named in (a). *(8L–9M)*

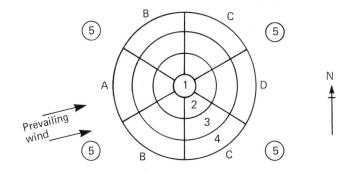

Prevailing wind

N

1. Central Business District
2. Transitional zone
3. Zone of small terrace houses in sectors C and D; larger bye-law housing in sector B, large old houses in sector A.
4. Post 1918 residential areas, with post 1945 development mainly on the periphery
5. Commuting distance 'dormitory' towns
A Middle–class sector
B Lower middle–class sector
C Working–class sector (and main council estates)
D Industry and lowest working–class sector

38

(a) How does the C.B.D. frame differ from the C.B.D. core? (9L–9M)

(b) Account for the clustering of similar commercial functions in the C.B.D. (9L–9M)

(c) Explain how such functional agglomeration can be measured. (7L–7M)

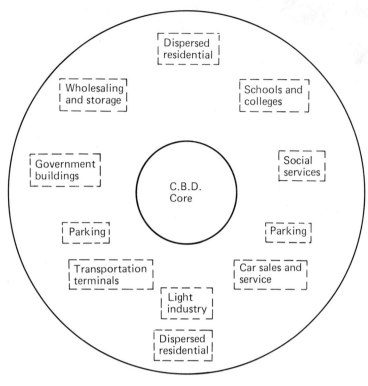

The C.B.D.: core and frame

39

(a) Account for the central location of commercial land uses. (6L–8M)

(b) Explain the different gradients of bid-rent for commercial and residential land uses. (8L–8M)

(c) Is the gradient for industry realistic in terms of the modern city? (8L–9M)

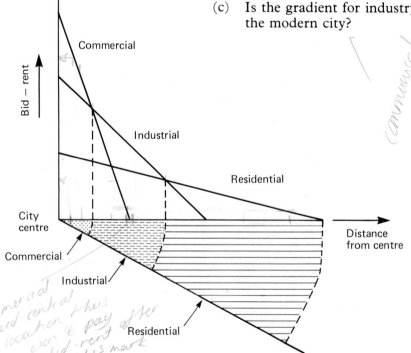

Idealised bid-rent curves for three land uses in a city

40

(a) What is meant by the term 'peak land value intersection'? (*3L–3M*)

(b) In which urban region are the highest land values concentrated? (*1L–2M*)

(c) Describe and explain the land use pattern in this region. (*10L–10M*)

(d) Account for the distribution of secondary land value peaks. (*10L–10M*)

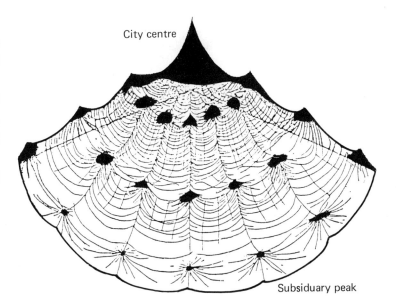

City centre

Subsiduary peak

41

(a) Give two reasons for the original location of the Jewish population near the city centre. (*2 × [3L–3M]*)

(b) Identify the likely factors which initiated the movements indicated. (*7L–7M*)

(c) Is there any noticeable pattern in the spread of the Jewish community? (*6L–6M*)

(d) How do residential areas generally differ between the inner city and areas further afield? (*6L–6M*)

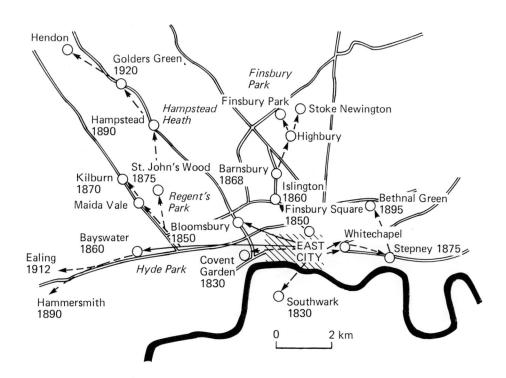

The spread of London's Jewish population from its point of origin east of the city

42

(a) What name is given to such a stage of urbanisation as that shown? *(1L–3M)*

(b) Account for the agglomeration of the individual communities. *(10L–10M)*

(c) Identify possible planning measures which can be used to prevent such development. *(12L–12M)*

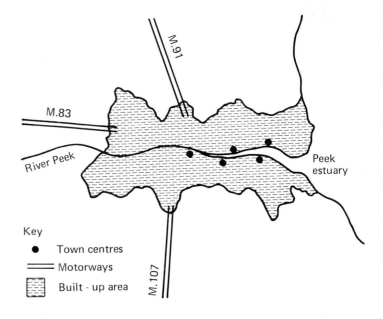

Key

●   Town centres

═══   Motorways

▨   Built - up area

43

(a) Why did Jean Gottman introduce the term 'megalopolis' to describe the extent of urbanisation along the north-eastern seaboard of the United States? *(5L–5M)*

(b) Isolate three factors which resulted in the formation of megalopolis. *(3 × [3L–4M])*

(c) Why has a megalopolis not evolved in the less developed world? *(10L–8M)*

The Megalopolis of the U.S. Atlantic Seaboard

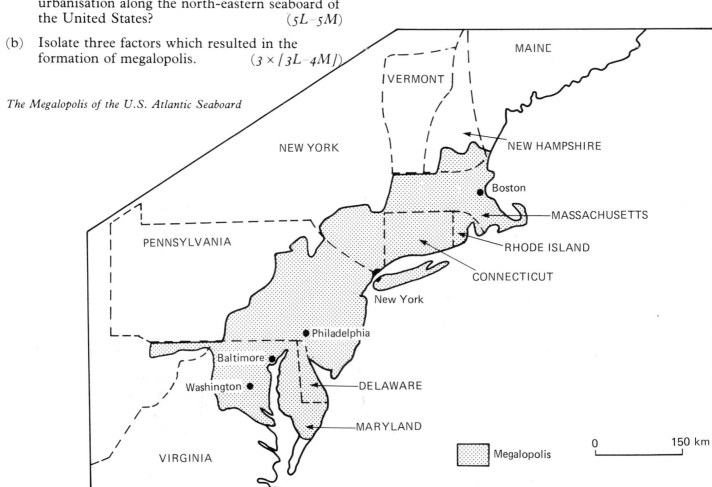

44

(a) Identify the changes illustrated by the model from colonial to post-colonial times. (6L–4M)

(b) Comment on the location of the industrial estate. (6L–6M)

(c) What major aspect of urban growth in the less developed world is not shown by the model? (4L–6M)

(d) With reference to one named example describe the other problems faced by cities in the less developed world. (10L–9M)

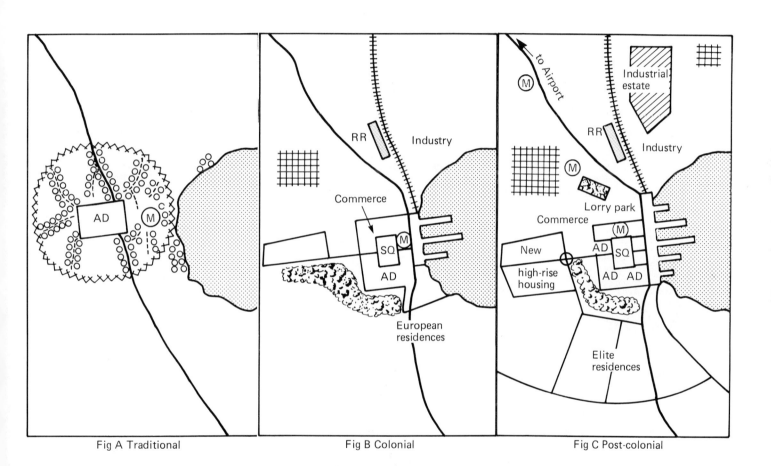

Fig A Traditional   Fig B Colonial   Fig C Post-colonial

Legend

ⅩⅣⅩⅣ Fortified wall	(M) Market	African housing developments
ₒ°ₒ Indigenous dwellings	SQ Square	---- Paths
Greenbelt	AD Administration	Major roads

Idealised structure of an African Port City

25

45

(a) Give two reasons to explain the high rate of car ownership in the outer city. *(8L–6M)*

(b) Explain the impact of a high level of car ownership on urban land use. *(10L–10M)*

(c) Identify the policies that a large metropolitan authority could pursue to reduce the intensity of traffic in the inner city. *(8L–9M)*

Households with at least one car as a percentage of all households

▨ 60.0 or more

☐ 50.0 – 59.9

▥ 40.0 – 49.9

▦ 30.0 – 39.9

☐ Less than 30.0

0   3 km

Car ownership

46

(a) List one region in each of three separate countries in the developed world where such a phenomenon has occurred in the 20th century. *(3L–6M)*

(b) Why are business services invariably reduced before social services? *(6L–6M)*

(c) How might local or regional government try to reverse such a trend? *(6L–6M)*

(d) For one named region or community detail the way in which rural depopulation has occurred. *(10L–7M)*

Model of the downward spiral of rural depopulation

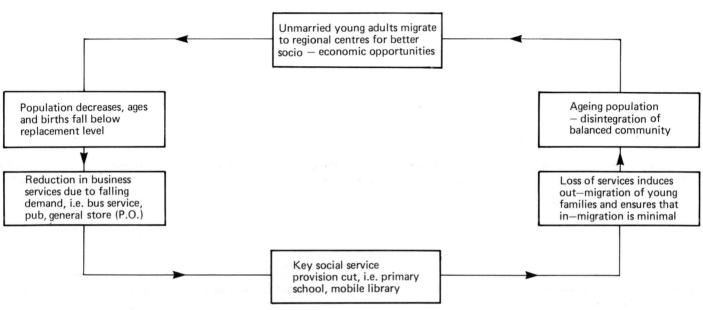

Unmarried young adults migrate to regional centres for better socio – economic opportunities

Population decreases, ages and births fall below replacement level

Ageing population – disintegration of balanced community

Reduction in business services due to falling demand, i.e. bus service, pub, general store (P.O.)

Loss of services induces out–migration of young families and ensures that in–migration is minimal

Key social service provision cut, i.e. primary school, mobile library

---

47

(a) (i) On a tracing of the diagram, using the letters A and B, mark the likely sites of two villages originally located in the medieval period. *(4M)*

    (ii) Justify the sites chosen *(6L–6M)*

(b) How would the settlements expand with modern population increase? *(5L–4M)*

(c) Examine 20th century changes in the socio-economic structure of villages in close proximity to large metropolitan areas. *(12L–11M)*

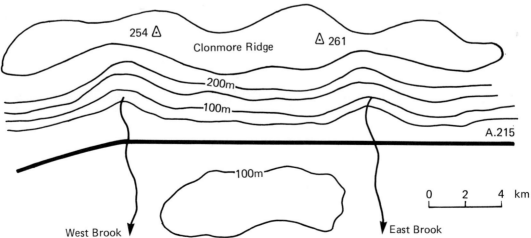

254 △ Clonmore Ridge △ 261

—200m—

—100m—

A.215

—100m—

0 2 4 km

Village location West Brook East Brook

Settlement Geography – Section B

48

(a)
(i) Which three regions of the less developed world had the highest percentage population living in urban areas in 1975? *(3M)*
(ii) Which three world regions had the greatest increase in urbanisation between 1950 and 1975? *(3M)*
(iii) Which three world regions are projected to register the greatest increases in urbanisation between 1975 and 2000? *(3M)*

(b) In what ways do heavily urbanised regions in the more developed world reflect population pressure? *(6M)*

(c) With reference to specific examples examine the problems which have resulted in both urban and rural areas from rapid urbanisation in the less developed world. *(10M)*

Proportions of population living in urban areas, by major areas and regions, 1950–2000 (Percentage)

	1950	1960	1970	1975	1980	1990	2000
World total	28.95	33.89	37.51	39.34	41.31	45.88	51.29
More developed regions	52.54	58.73	64.68	67.49	70.15	74.87	78.75
Less developed regions	16.71	21.85	25.82	28.03	30.53	36.46	43.46
Africa	14.54	18.15	22.85	25.67	28.85	35.70	42.49
Eastern Africa	5.50	7.54	10.69	13.20	16.14	22.72	29.41
Middle Africa	14.57	18.10	25.16	29.66	34.37	43.65	51.36
Northern Africa	24.51	29.77	36.61	40.12	43.83	51.39	58.34
Southern Africa	37.27	41.70	43.76	44.81	46.49	51.43	57.90
Western Africa	10.15	13.48	17.27	19.58	22.29	28.65	35.92
Latin America	41.18	49.45	57.37	61.21	64.74	70.70	75.21
Caribbean	33.51	38.22	45.08	48.62	52.15	58.74	64.62
Middle America	39.75	46.71	53.88	57.37	60.75	66.95	72.17
Temperate South America	64.77	72.74	77.87	80.16	82.18	85.45	87.83
Tropical South America	36.29	46.36	56.05	60.70	64.85	71.52	76.17
Northern America	63.84	67.09	70.45	71.99	73.66	77.20	80.76
East Asia	16.72	24.71	28.61	30.70	33.05	38.63	45.43
China	11.00	18.60	21.60	23.29	25.41	31.07	38.61
Japan	50.20	62.40	71.30	75.08	78.24	82.93	85.86
Other East Asia	28.61	36.31	47.46	53.43	58.85	67.51	73.03
South Asia	15.65	17.80	20.45	22.02	23.95	29.10	36.13
Eastern South Asia	14.83	17.52	20.02	21.38	23.15	28.10	35.10
Middle South Asia	15.59	17.19	19.40	20.77	22.53	27.48	34.48
Western South Asia	23.38	32.52	44.48	50.45	55.75	63.49	68.50
Europe	53.70	58.42	63.94	66.45	68.83	73.25	77.11
Eastern Europe	41.48	47.90	53.26	56.26	59.31	65.23	70.56
Northern Europe	74.32	76.73	81.28	83.32	85.12	87.95	89.92
Southern Europe	41.01	46.15	52.90	56.25	59.41	65.26	70.31
Western Europe	63.92	69.20	74.38	76.25	78.08	81.36	84.27
Oceania	61.24	66.22	70.77	73.35	75.93	80.37	82.97
U.S.S.R.	39.30	48.80	56.70	60.90	64.77	71.28	76.06

49

(a) According to the Murphy and Vance method, to qualify as part of the C.B.D. a block must have a C.B.H.I. of 1.0 or more and a C.B.I.I. in excess of 50%. From the block profile provided calculate whether Block X forms part of the C.B.D. *(9M)*

(b) Assess the merits and limitations of this method of delimiting the C.B.D. *(4M)*

(c) Briefly describe three other criteria which might be used to assess the boundaries of the C.B.D. *(6M)*

(d) Outline three ways in which the C.B.D. might change to cater for a rapidly rising and increasingly affluent local population. *(6M)*

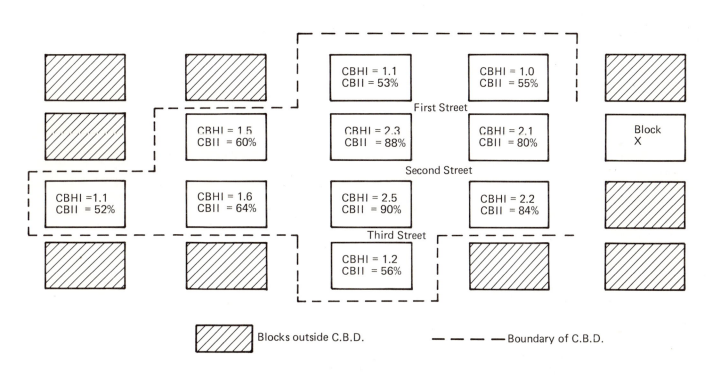

CBHI = 1.1 CBII = 53%			CBHI = 1.0 CBII = 55%		

First Street

CBHI = 1.5 CBII = 60%	CBHI = 2.3 CBII = 88%	CBHI = 2.1 CBII = 80%	Block X

Second Street

CBHI = 1.1 CBII = 52%	CBHI = 1.6 CBII = 64%	CBHI = 2.5 CBII = 90%	CBHI = 2.2 CBII = 84%

Third Street

CBHI = 1.2 CBII = 56%

Blocks outside C.B.D. — — — Boundary of C.B.D.

Central Business Height Index = $\dfrac{\text{Total number of C.B.D. units in block}}{\text{Total number of ground floor units}}$

Central Business Intensity Index = $\dfrac{\text{Total number of C.B.D. units in block}}{\text{Total number of units in block}} \times \dfrac{1}{100}$

Block X

X	X	X	X	X	C	X	X
C	C	C	X	X	C	C	C
C	C	C	X	X	C	C	C

C = C.B.D. units (i.e. shops, offices, restaurants)
X = Non - C.B.D. units (i.e. residential, storage, vacant)

50

(a) Identify (i) the advantages and (ii) the disadvantages of building a new capital city at Abuja. *(2 × [3M])*

(b) If the plan went ahead what economic advantages might Lagos maintain over Abuja? *(4M)*

(c) What effects might a successful new capital city have on (i) the transport network of the country, (ii) the distribution of population and (iii) the land use within the daily zone of influence of the capital? *(3 × [3M])*

(d) Describe the main elements of planning of one such previous scheme. *(6M)*

NIGERIA

Next year in Abuja?

FROM OUR LAGOS CORRESPONDENT

Nigeria's quest for a new capital city is causing acute friction among its politicians. The two chambers of the national assembly are now at loggerheads over the proposal to move the capital next year to Abuja, in the centre of the country. The senate has voted unanimously against the move; the house of representatives is strongly for it.

To Nigeria's present rulers, shifting the federal capital offers two undeniable advantages. The first is an escape from the traffic jams, electricity and water cuts, overcrowding and armed robberies of Lagos. At Abuja, 300 miles to the north-east, the proposed new capital would be purpose-built and landscaped, like Canberra or Brasilia.

Its other advantage would be that it is well away from Yorubaland—whereas Lagos is in the heart of the Yorubas' territory, which the ruling National party regards as an opposition stronghold. The proposed move thus represents an escape from the south by the northern-dominated ruling party as well as part of the search for the unity that Nigeria, in 21 years of independence, has never really achieved.

The Yoruba-dominated Unity party is, naturally, Abuja's most outspoken opponent. It regards the plan to move the capital as an irresponsible waste of resources that could have been used to improve the living conditions of the 4m inhabitants of Lagos. However, such criticism has had no effect on the federal government. Abuja was spared when large expenditure cuts were announced in September as a result of Nigeria's poor oil production figures. Unity party members complain that $9 billion has already been spent on Abuja and that much of this has vanished without producing visible results. They are demanding an investigation of how the money was spent.

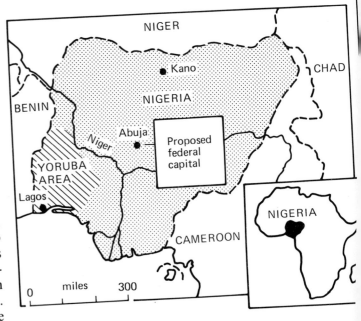

51

(a) How important have communications been to the location and development of Crawley new town? (5M)

(b) Explain the location of industry in the town. (5M)

(c) What are the likely advantages and disadvantages of Gatwick airport to the town? (6M)

(d) Describe four characteristics of the neighbourhood principle upon which housing is based. (6M)

(e) What is the difference between a new town and an expanded town? (3M)

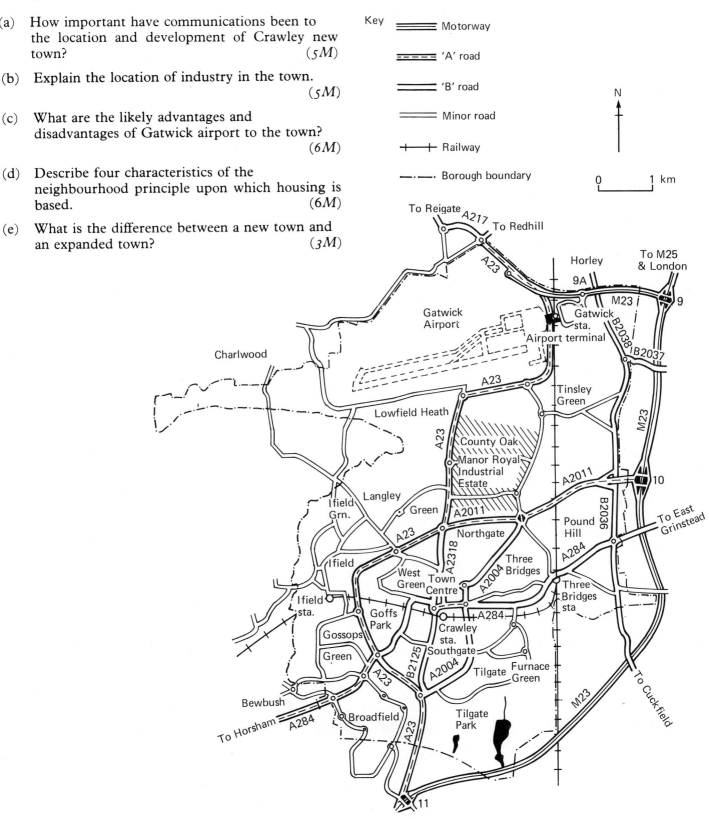

Map of Crawley Borough

52

(a) Describe the distribution of noise in the City of Toronto. (*4M*)

(b) What are the likely factors responsible for sound levels in excess of 70 dBA? (*5M*)

(c) Which types of land use are likely to dominate those areas with sound levels below 60 dBA? (*5M*)

(d) Which of the high sound level regions have probably achieved that status most recently? Indicate why. (*5M*)

(e) What other factors would have to be taken into account to arrive at an index of urban nuisance? (*6M*)

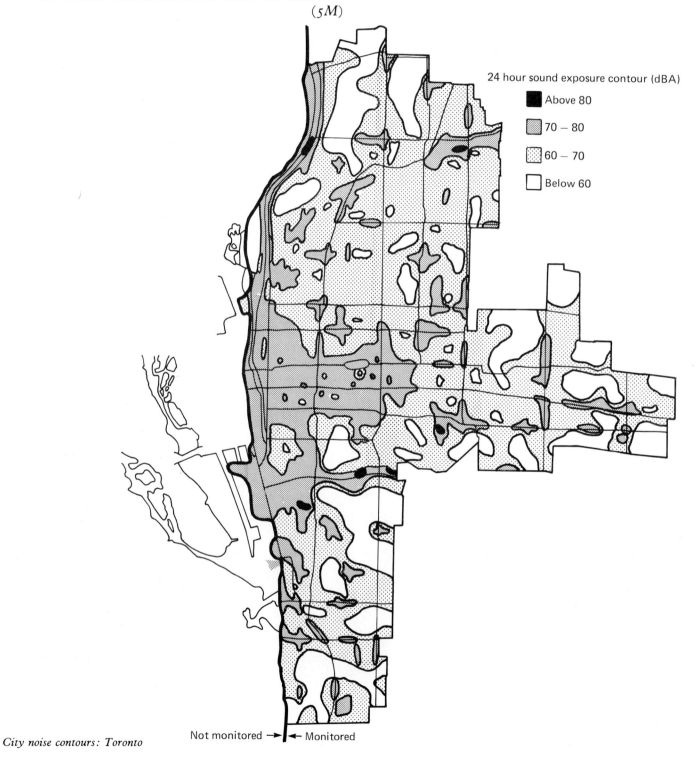

24 hour sound exposure contour (dBA)

■ Above 80

▨ 70 — 80

▧ 60 — 70

□ Below 60

Not monitored → | ← Monitored

City noise contours: Toronto

53

(a) Describe the variations in per capita Rate Support Grant shown by the map. (4M)

(b) How important is government assistance of this nature to inner city areas? (6M)

(c) What other measures have been used or suggested to prevent the demise of the inner city? (7M)

(d) How far does the model help to explain the problems faced by inner city regions? (8M)

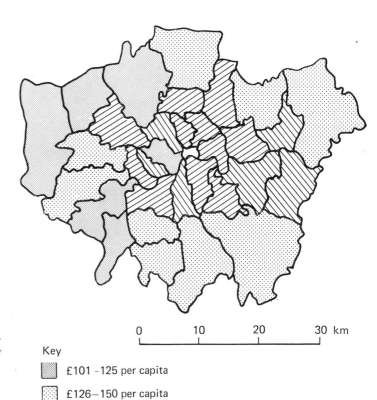

Greater London: Rate Support Grant per capita, 1979/80 allocation.

The Rate Support Grant is paid from central government funds to supplement rate income for rating authorities. As such it provides a reasonable measure of need.

Key
- £101 –125 per capita
- £126 –150 per capita
- £151 –175 per capita
- £176 and over

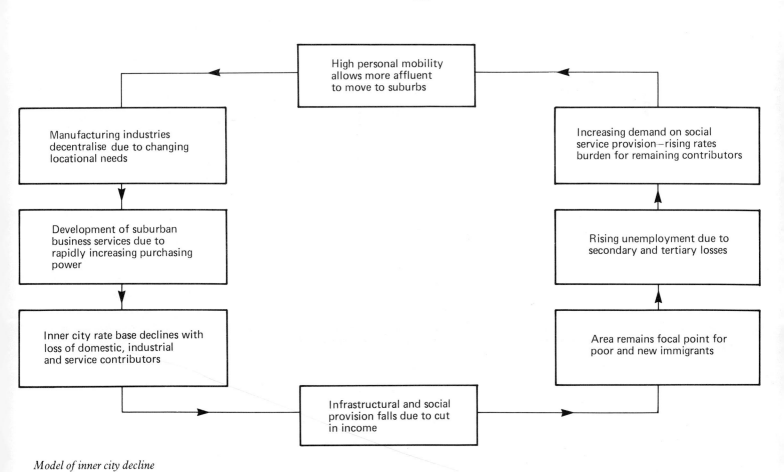

Model of inner city decline

54

(a) Briefly explain the meaning of the following terms in the context of the model: (i) peripheral accretion, (ii) linear development, (iii) leap-frogging. (3M)

(b) Why do units of land ownership decrease in size but increase in value with proximity to the built-up area? (5M)

(c) Account for the contrasting rates of change in land ownership in the three zones shown in the model. (6M)

(d) What effects might ensuing urbanization have on agriculture in the rural-urban fringe? (6M)

(e) What kind of planning measures could be implemented to prevent the chaotic sprawl of the urban area? (5M)

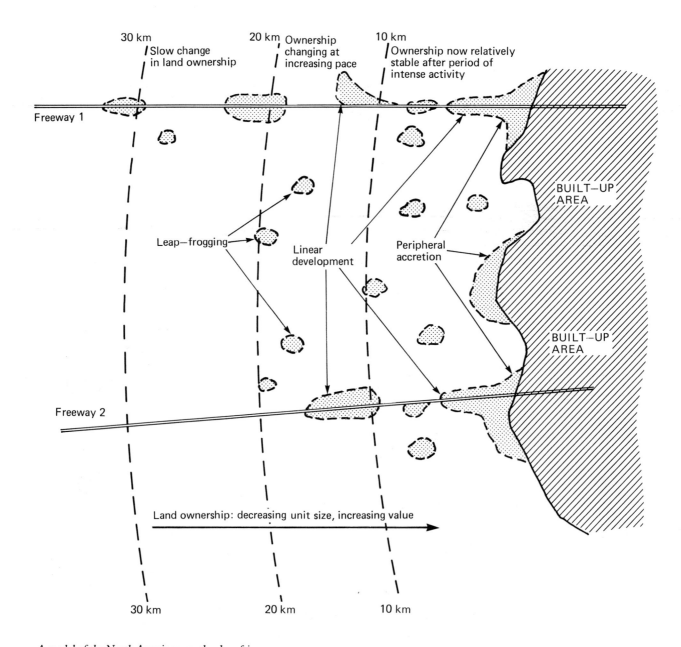

A model of the North American rural-urban fringe

Economic Geography – Section A

55

(a) What are the usual titles given to Stages 3 and 4? (2L–4M)

(b) Name an example of a country which approximates the conditions in: (i) Stage 2, (ii) Stage 3, (iii) Stage 4 and (iv) Stage 5. (4L–4M)

(c) Compare the structures of manufacturing Industry that might be expected in Stages 2 and 5. (10L–8M)

(d) How far can the model be regarded as a blueprint for development in the less developed world? (10L–9M)

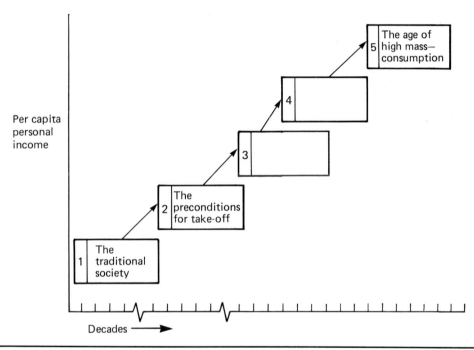

56

(a) Why do major sub-cores tend to develop at a substantial distance from the core region? (6L–7M)

(b) Compare the core and periphery in terms of the following: (i) Manufacturing industry (ii) Infrastructure (iii) Demographic characteristics. (3 × [5L–4M])

(c) How might a smaller sub-core develop into a major sub-core? (5L–6M)

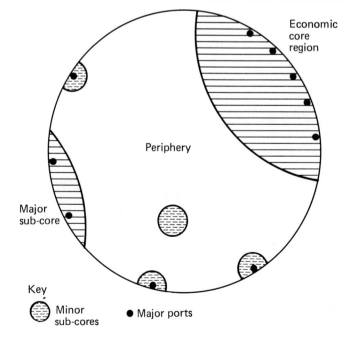

57

(a) The terms (i) Spread effects and (ii) Backwash effects form an important part of the theory of cumulative causation. Explain each term.

(2 × [5L–4M])

(b) In a free economy would the process of cumulative causation tend to increase or decrease regional inequalities? (9L–9M)

(c) What has been the general aim of government intervention in regard to regional economic development? (6L–8M)

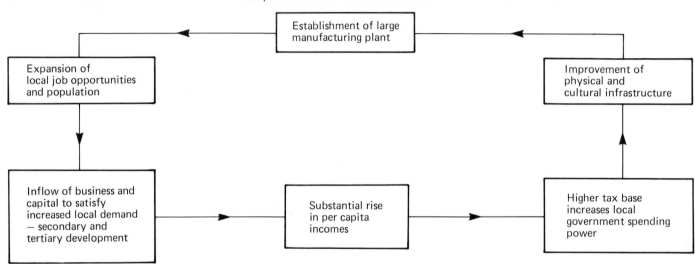

Simplified model of cumulative causation

58

(a) Suggest reasons for the expansion of key ports. (5L–6M)

(b) Explain the development of (i) feeder routes, (ii) Intermediate nodes on major routeways and (iii) High priority highways. (3 × [3L–3M])

(c) Why does the transport network in many developing countries only approximate Stage 2 or Stage 3? (10L–10M)

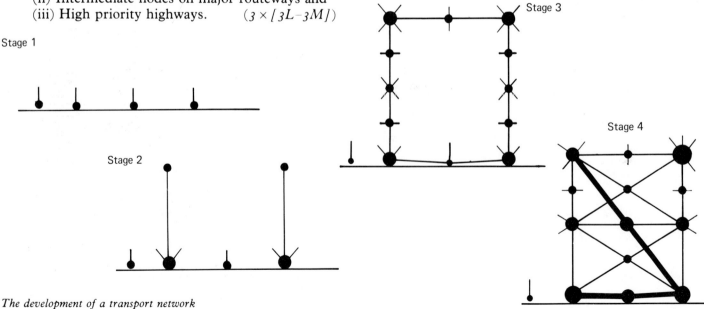

The development of a transport network

59

(a) (i) F requires more direct links to A and G to
     sustain recent economic growth. On a
     tracing of the diagram draw in two ways
     how this could be achieved.   (6M)

     (ii) Examine the factors which might support
     the adoption of each proposal.   (8L–8M)

(b) (i) Which single new link would best increase
     the economic accessibility of H?   (1L–3M)

     (ii) What information would be required to
     assess the feasibility of such a link?
                                          (8L–8M)

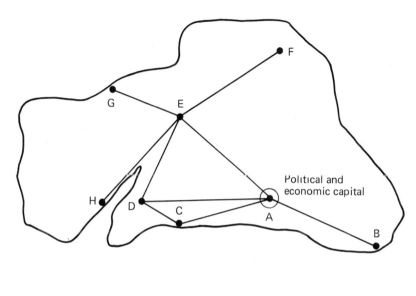

● Regional centres   —— Motorway network

                            —— Coastline

60

(a) Using the Beta Index, formula E/V, calculate the
    connectivity of (i) network A and (ii) network B.
                                    (2 × [1L–4M])

(b) Identify two factors which might account for the
    low connectivity of B.   (2 × [3L–3M])

(c) How can a low connectivity transport network
    affect economic development?   (11L–11M)

Road network A

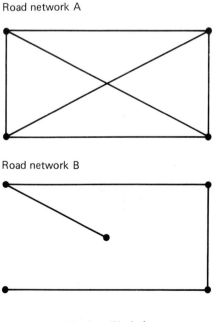

Road network B

—— Edges   ● Vertices (Nodes)

61

(a) Identify three factors which may have contributed to the decline of the railways. *(3 × [3L–4M])*

(b) Account for the low proportion of freight carried by air transport. *(4L–4M)*

(c) Suggest how the relative importance of these modes of transport might differ for intercity passenger traffic. *(10L–9M)*

Volume of domestic intercity freight traffic 1950 and 1978

Mode	1950	1978
	%	%
Railways	57.4	35.8
Road transport	15.8	24.8
Inland waterways	14.9	15.8
Pipelines	11.8	23.4
Air transport	0.029	0.2
Total traffic volume (billions of tonne miles)	1094	2425

The table shows the mode of intercity freight traffic in 1950 and 1978 for a developed country.

62

(a) Suggest the most likely reasons for:
  (i) The relative decline of coal between 1960 and 1979. *(6L–4M)*
  (ii) Its projected increase by 1990. *(4L–4M)*

(b) Identify three factors which might delay or postpone the development of nuclear power. *(3 × [3L–3M])*

(c) What are the difficulties involved in expanding H.E.P. in most developed countries? *(6L–8M)*

Energy supply for a developed country

Source	1960	1979	1990 estimate
	%	%	%
H.E.P. + others	3.7	3.8	3.3
Nuclear	–	3.8	10.5
Coal	21.9	19.3	26.3
Gas	29.7	25.6	18.5
Oil	44.7	47.5	41.4

63

(a) On a tracing of the diagram mark clearly (i) The least-cost location, (ii) The margins of profitability and (iii) Non-profitable locations. *(7M)*

(b) Explain three ways by which the margin of profitability could be extended. *(3 × [3L–2M])*

(c) Identify three factors which might deflect the siting of a factory from the least-cost location. *(3 × [3L–4M])*

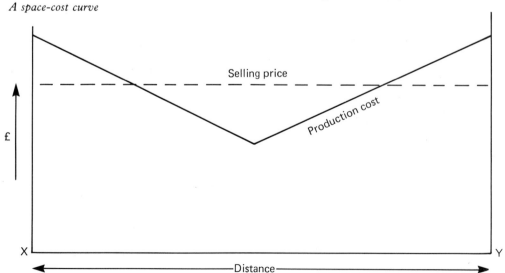

A space-cost curve

The diagram shows that production costs vary with location.

64

(a) (i) On a tracing of the diagram insert the 8 and 9 unit isodapanes. (ii) Shade in the zone of least cost location. (*10M*)

(b) Examine the effect of the following on plant location: (i) Weight loss in manufacture,

(ii) Sources of relatively cheap labour and (iii) Agglomeration economies. (*3 × [5L–5M]*)

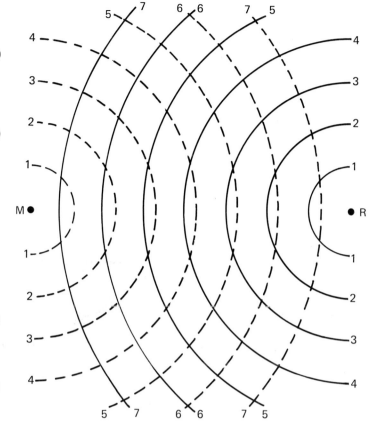

----- Costs of transporting finished product to market (M)

——— Costs of transporting raw material from source (R)

65

(a) (i) According to Weber which factor is the primary determinant of plant location. (*1L–3M*)

(ii) If Y = plant location, Z = market, what are X_1 and X_2? (*1L–2M*)

(iii) What do the terms weight loss and weight gain mean? (*6L–6M*)

(b) Identify the factors which could 'pull' plant location to each corner of the triangle. (*6L–6M*)

(c) State four assumptions upon which the model is based. (*4 × [2L–2M]*)

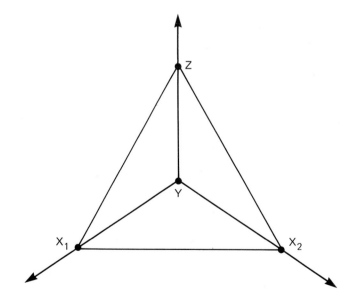

Weber's Weight Triangle

66

(a) Explain the terms: (i) Product cycle and (ii) External economies. $(2 \times [4L-3M])$

(b) Explain the importance of the major production factors in: (i) the early phase and (ii) the mature phase. $(2 \times [5L-5M])$

(c) How might the changing importance of production factors influence industrial location? $(8L-9M)$

The relative importance of various production factors in different phases of the product cycle (in rank order of importance)

Production factors		Management	Scientific — engineering knowhow	Unskilled labour	External economies	Capital
Product cycle phase	Early	2	1	3	1	3
	Growth	1	2	2	2	1ª
	Mature	3	3	1	3	1ª

67

(a) Explain the terms: (i) Vertical integration (ii) Horizontal integration. $(2 \times [4L-4M])$

(b) Identify the factors which promote the interregional expansion of an industrial enterprise. $(10L-10M)$

(c) Explain the transition from one product specialisation to multiproduct manufacture. $(6L-7M)$

Stages of a Firm's Reorganisation

Stage	Products	Plants	Location	Market	Processes
1	One	One	One city	One region	One
2	One	One	One city	One region	Multiprocess (vertical)
3	One	One	One city	Multiregion	Multiprocess (vertical)
4	One	Multiplant	Multicity	Multiregion	Multiprocess (vertical)
5	Multiproduct	Multiplant	Multicity	Multiregion	Multiprocess (vertical)
6	Multiproduct	Multiplant	Multicity	Multiregion	Multiprocess (vertical – horizontal)

68

(a) Under what circumstances might the frontier of settlement be extended northwards? *(8L–10M)*

(b) Assess the likely economic, demographic and infrastructural characteristics of such new settlements. *(12L–10M)*

(c) How permanent do such settlements tend to be? *(6L–5M)*

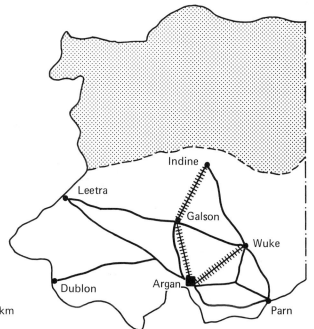

Key

■ Capital city and major port

● Other major settlements

++++ Railways

— Major roads

—·—· International border

- - - Northern limit of permanent road network

▦ Virtually uninhabited land

0 100 200 km

69

(a) (i) What is meant by 'locational rent' (economic rent)? *(4L–5M)*
   (ii) On a tracing of the diagram clearly mark the margin of cultivation for each of the three crops. *(3M)*

(b) Give two ways in which the margin of cultivation of crop A could be extended. *(6L–8M)*

(c) How far does the model of locational rent explain the distribution of intensive and extensive farming? *(10L–9M)*

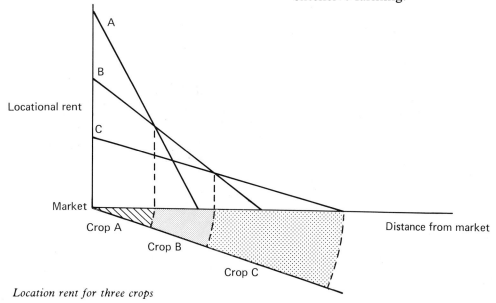

Location rent for three crops

70

(a) Describe the distribution of land use around the village. *(6L–6M)*

(b) Comment on the possible factors governing this pattern of land use. *(8L–10M)*

(c) What conditions might lead to an extension of one land use at the expense of the other two? *(10L–9M)*

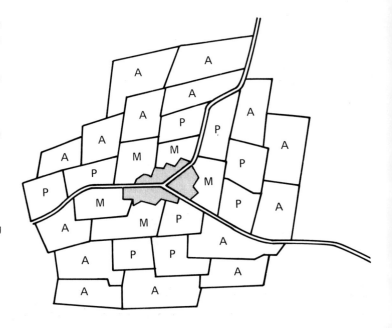

Key

▨ Village

M   Market gardening
P   Pasture
A   Arable

Land use around Codswallop village

71

(a) Explain the terms: (i) Economic margin, (ii) Economic limit and (iii) Physical limit. *(3 × [3L–3M])*

(b) Under what circumstances might cultivation be pushed beyond the economic margin? *(7L–8M)*

(c) Examine the ways in which the physical limits to cultivation have been overcome in one named region. *(8L–8M)*

Too hot

Yield

0
10
20
30
40
50
60

Optimum

3
4
5
7
10
20
∞

Cost

Too cold

Temperature   Too dry

Too wet

Rainfall

Key

⎯⎯ Physical limit

⎯ ⎯ Economic limit

.... Economic margin

72

(a) Account for the location of branch plants and parent plants. (8L–7M)

(b) Identify four factors which have led to parent plants themselves relocating in 'green field' sites. (4 × [3L–2M])

(c) What advantages and disadvantages might plant W1 bring to the local community? (8L–10M)

Key

◩ Central city

▦ Suburban region

● Parent plant

■ Branch plant

— Major roads

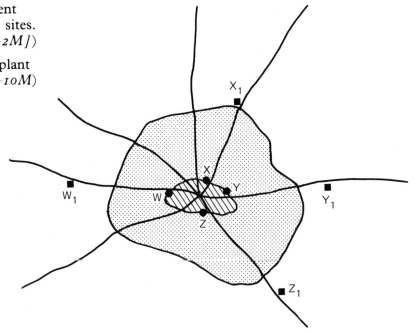

73

(a) Factory A may be relocated to compensate for changing economic circumstances. On a tracing of the diagram mark on the most economic new location. (3M)

(b) Identify three factors which might sway the decision-makers against closure of factory A. (3 × [4L–4M])

(c) What effects might relocation have on (i) the recipient area? (ii) the area of plant closure? (2 × [6L–5M])

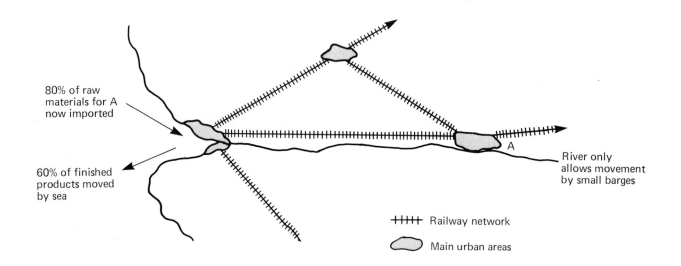

80% of raw materials for A now imported

60% of finished products moved by sea

River only allows movement by small barges

┼┼┼┼ Railway network

⬭ Main urban areas

74

(a) Comment on the relationship between per capita energy demand and per capita gross national product. (5L–5M)

(b) What is the approximate total daily energy demand of (i) the United States and (ii) the Far East? (2L–6M)

(c) Suggest why Canada has a higher energy demand but a significantly lower per capita G.N.P. than the United States. (6L–5M)

(d) What effect might rapid economic development in the three poorer continents have on the world energy situation? (12L–9M)

	Per capita energy demand barrels/day oil equivalent/ person	Per capita gross national product 1979 $ / person*	Population millions of persons
United States	.18	11 000	220
Canada	.19	9 400	24
Europe	.07	8 700	370
Middle East	.02	2 700	135
C.P.E.	.03	1 800	1391
Latin America	.02	1 600	352
Far East	.01	1 200	1395
Africa	.01	700	417
World	.03	2 600	4304

*Estimated

Energy demand and Gross National Product per capita, 1979

75

(a) (i) Identify the main regions with poor motorway provision. (2L–3M)
   (ii) Account for this situation (7L–5M)

(b) Name the focal points of the network in the country as a whole. (2L–3M)

(c) List three simple statistical measures by which regional contrasts could be recognised. (3L–6M)

(d) Assess the economic impact of poor road transport provision. (10L–8M)

Key

M85 ▬ Motorways open

A23 ═ Main primary routes

Preston ○ Principal towns

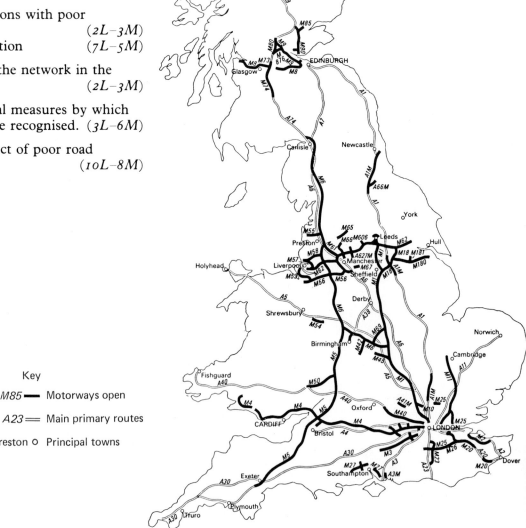

British motorway network

76

(a) Identify the three regions where
(i) Manufacturing industry is relatively most important (ii) Tertiary occupations are relatively most important. $(2 \times [2L - 3M])$

(b) Account for the varied employment structure indicated by the map. $(10L - 11M)$

(c) Explain (i) the changes that have occurred in the last two decades (ii) the changes that are likely in the next two decades. $(10L - 8M)$

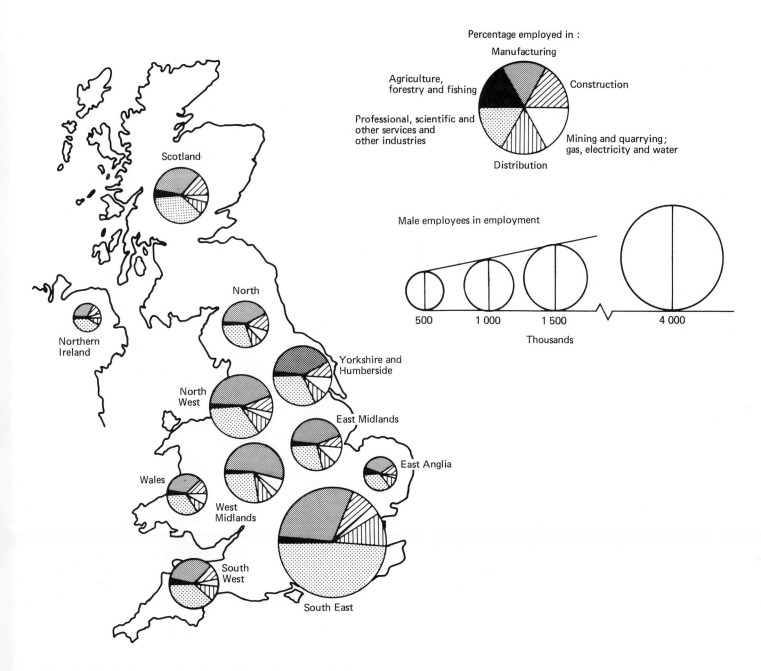

Industrial distribution of male employees in employment, 1980

77

(a) The late 1970's has been a period of marked recession for world shipbuilding:
  (i) Identify the countries which have been most successful in maintaining production.

  (3L–3M)

  (ii) Attempt to explain why this has been so.

  (8L–8M)

(b) How important is the level of world trade to the shipbuilding industry? *(6L–6M)*

(c) For one region in a developed country assess the consequences of decline in the region's shipyards. *(10L–8M)*

World shipbuilding – merchant vessels launched (Thousands of gross registered tons)

	WORLD	Belgium	Brazil	Canada	Denmark	Finland	France	Germany Fed. Rep.	Greece	India	Italy	Japan
1974	34 624	217	319	142	1125	204	1343	2109	141	41	868	17 584
1975	34 203	212	389	206	983	256	1315	2545	76	45	843	17 740
1976	33 922	184	426	237	948	389	1208	1786	76	55	664	14 524
1977	27 532	169	572	208	633	324	1148	1373	85	37	688	9 838
1978	18 194	266	442	135	399	293	644	599	25	54	184	4 801
1979	11 458	126	665	177	199	230	728	374	26	30	148	4 249
1980	13 572	415	625	75	225	200	328	461	22	74	167	7 308

	Korea, Rep. of	Netherlands	Norway	Poland	Portugal	Singapore	Spain	Sweden	Turkey	United Kingdom	United States	Yugoslavia
1974	445	722	998	589	96	49	1426	2214	16	1262	810	777
1975	435	944	1035	617	165	84	1633	2470	28	1294	1006	639
1976	674	578	756	518	252	86	1624	2367	13	1347	1047	583
1977	463	380	530	492	17	117	1568	2127	49	1124	1038	285
1978	402	202	354	679	183	54	643	1305	28	814	913	242
1979	441	183	260	489	176	62	512	461	51	608	706	173
1980	626	125	315	393	167	27	510	326	15	242	547	123

78

(a) Account for the general decline in the average daily concentrations of smoke and sulphur dioxide. *(8L–8M)*

(b) Attempt to explain the regional variations in 1978/79. *(9L–9M)*

(c) How far are the trends illustrated by the table characteristic of the less developed world? *(8L–8M)*

Smoke and Sulphur dioxide: trends in national and regional average daily concentrations at urban sites 1968/69–1978/79 (Micrograms per cubic metre)

	Smoke			Sulphur dioxide		
	1968/69	1973/74	1978/79	1968/69	1973/74	1978/79
North	111	55	25	101	72	49
Yorkshire and Humberside	98	44	35	144	89	74
East Midlands	80	44	30	106	77	69
East Anglia	51	35	20	87	66	49
Greater London	46	36	24	152	118	82
South East (excluding Greater London)	39	27	17	81	64	51
South West	35	24	16	59	49	43
West Midlands	63	39	28	119	77	70
North West	110	49	28	149	93	75
England	74	40	26	124	84	66
Wales	40	30	18	56	69	49
Scotland	85	35	25	84	65	50
Northern Ireland	79	53	35	95	72	35
United Kingdom	74	39	26	118	81	62

The regional averages are not based on precisely the same sites, so the figures are not strictly comparable between years.

79

(a) The level of petroleum hydrocarbons in European waters has increased considerably in recent decades. Itemise four major reasons for such an increase. *(4 × [2L–2M])*

(b) What is meant by (i) urban runoff, (ii) natural seeps? *(2 × [3L–2M])*

(c) For one named developed country state the locations of its major coastal refineries. *(4L–6M)*

(d) Discuss pollution control measures which could reduce the level of petroleum hydrocarbons in oceans. *(10L–7M)*

Petroleum hydrocarbons in the oceans

Source	Million tonnes per annum.
Offshore oil production	0.1
Transportation (tankers, dry docking, terminal operations, bilges, accidents)	2.1
Coastal refineries, municipal and industrial waste	0.8
River and urban runoff	1.9
Atmospheric fallout	0.6
Natural seeps	0.6

Economic Geography – Section B

80

(a) (i) Explain the distinction between a Development Area, a Special Development Area and an Intermediate Area. (*4M*)

   (ii) Which economic regions in Great Britain were not in receipt of regional development grants in 1979/80? (*2M*)

(b) To what extent does the map help to explain the information given in the table? What additional information, if any, might be required for a more detailed analysis? (*7M*)

(c) Following current trends, what changes are likely to occur to the picture presented by the map by 1989? (*4M*)

(d) The Northern region received the greatest allocation of regional development grants in 1979/80. What other forms of investment might be necessary in the region to ensure the efficient use of the money allocated to plant and machinery, buildings and works? (*8M*)

⊡ Agriculture, forestry and fishing
⊞ Manufacturing
⊟ Construction
⊞ Mining and quarrying ; gas, electricity and water
⊠ Transport and communications, distributive trades
☐ Professional, scientific and misc. services
■ Insurance, banking and finance, ownership of dwellings, public administration and defence, adjustment for financial services

 = 5%

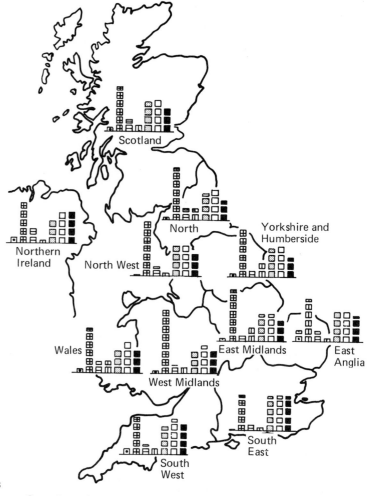

Gross domestic product by broad industry group, 1979

Regional development grants (1) paid in 1979/80 (£ million)

	Total plant and machinery, building and works	Plant and machinery			Building works				
		Special development areas	Development areas	Total plant and machinery	Special development areas	Development areas	Inter-mediate areas	Derelict land clearance areas	Total building and works
Great Britain	330.8	115.5	124.6	240.1	27.2	34.1	29.4	–	90.7
North	122.4	40.4	56.9	97.3	9.5	15.6	–	–	25.1
Yorkshire and Humberside	21.5	–	7.4	7.4	–	2.5	11.6	–	14.1
East Midlands	2.4	–	–	–	–	–	2.4	–	2.4
South West	5.0	–	2.9	2.9	–	1.3	0.8	–	2.1
West Midlands	–	–	–	–	–	–	–	–	–
North West	58.7	37.5	–	37.5	8.6	–	12.6	–	21.2
England	210.0	77.9	67.2	145.1	18.1	19.4	27.4	–	64.9
Wales	50.7	8.7	31.6	40.3	1.5	7.8	1.1	–	10.4
Scotland	70.1	28.9	25.8	54.7	7.6	6.9	0.9	–	15.4

(1) Grants paid under the Industry Act 1972

81

(a) The map shows the intercity passenger rail network of the United States and the table the connectivity of the network for 7 of the 9 major census divisions of the country. Complete the table by calculating the Beta Index for the Pacific and West South Central divisions (the junction of a route with a divisional boundary should be counted as a vertice.)   (9M)

(b) Using the table and by consulting an atlas assess the relationship between population distribution and passenger rail connectivity.   (4M)

(c) What other information would be required to gain a comprehensive picture of the intercity rail passenger service?   (6M)

(d) How far does relief and drainage appear to have affected routeways?   (6M)

Division	Population 1980	Connectivity of passenger rail network – Beta Index 1980
New England	12.35M	0.88
Middle Atlantic	36.79M	0.89
East North Central	41.67M	1.09
South Atlantic	36.31M	1.12
East South Central	14.66M	0.50
West South Central	23.74M	
West North Central	17.18M	0.71
Mountain	11.37M	0.77
Pacific	31.80M	

Divisions

1	New England	4	South Atlantic	7	West North Central
2	Middle Atlantic	5	East South Central	8	Mountain
3	East North Central	6	West South Central	9	Pacific

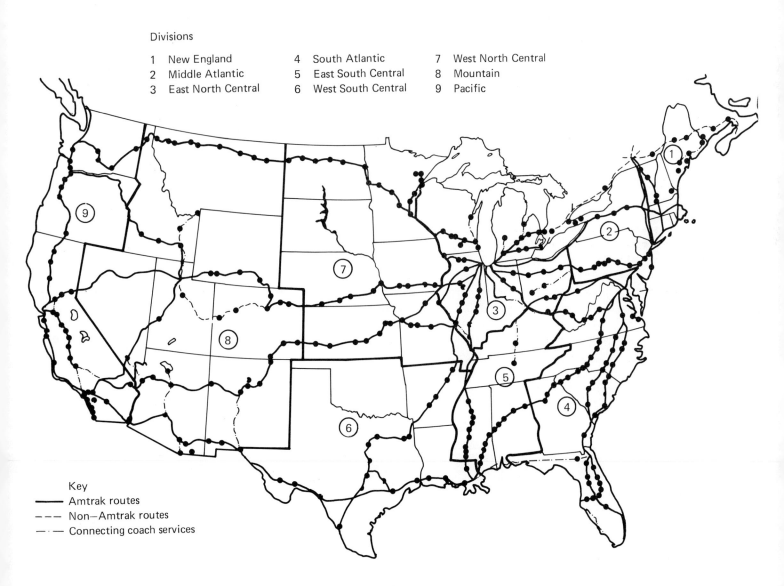

Key
——— Amtrak routes
– – – Non–Amtrak routes
– · – Connecting coach services

U.S. inter-city passenger rail routes

82

(a) Study the map and, with the aid of an atlas, complete the transport development matrix for the region beyond 65°N. *(8M)*

(b) What mathematical argument is there against using such sectors? Suggest a way in which such a disadvantage could be overcome. *(3M)*

(c) Describe and explain the spatial and temporal patterns indicated by the matrix. *(8M)*

(d) Assess the relative importance of rail, highway and air transport to the Canadian Northlands. *(6M)*

The Canadian Northlands

The figures show the number of airports handling scheduled flights in each sector. The words Road and/or Rail are written in those sectors which have these modes of transport.

		140°	130°	120°	110°	100°	90°	80°	70°	60°W	Total
75°N	1980										
	1965										0
	1955										0
70°N	1980	Road									
	1965	5	2	2	1						10
	1955	4	2								6
65°N	1980	Road Rail 4	Road 4	Road Rail 4		5	1	8	4		30
	1965	3	4	5					1		13
	1955	3	4	5							12
60°N	1980	Road Rail	Road Rail 4	Road Rail 5	Rail 7	Rail 5	2	4	3		30
	1965		5	4	16	2	1	1	1		30
	1955		4	4	13	1					22
55°N											

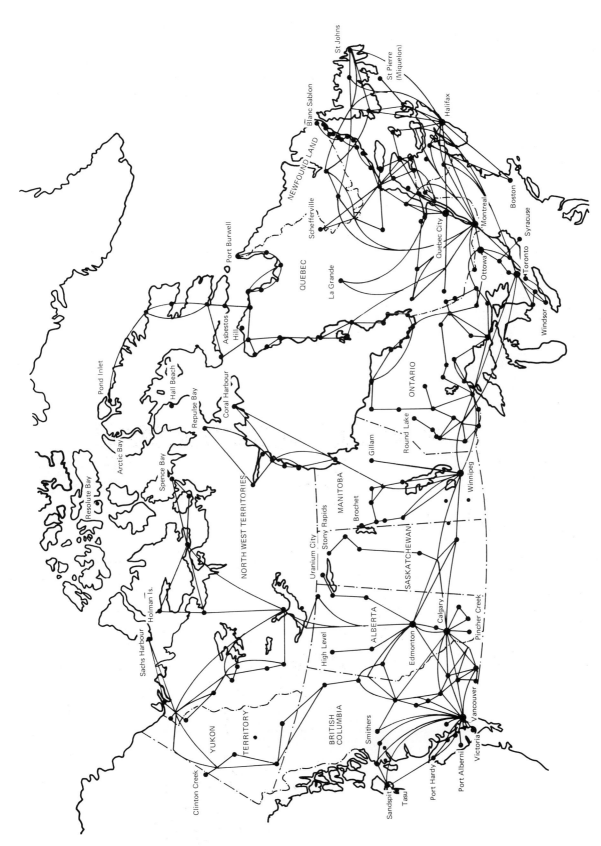

Canadian local air routes. Resolute Bay, Arctic Bay, Hall Beach and Asbestos Hill are on trunk routes

83

(a) By reference to an atlas locate the air basins with the greatest density of population and name the largest metropolitan areas within them. *(3M)*

(b) Assess the relationship between total generating capacity and total population by air basin. *(4M)*

·(c) Attempt to explain the basic variations in the type of electricity generation by air basin. *(7M)*

(d) Comment on the actual and potential environmental effects of each source of generation. *(7M)*

(e) Which air basins are likely to experience the greatest expansion in electricity generation in the coming decades? *(4M)*

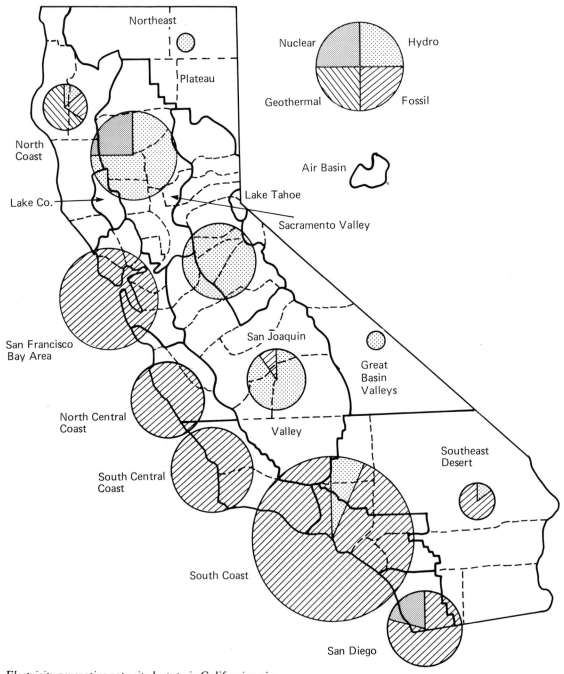

Electricity generating capacity by type in Californian air basins in 1976

84

(a) State three differences, including relevant figures deduced from the map, between the location of (British) North Sea oil and North Sea gas. (*3M*)

(b) Explain how these differences have affected the economics of production. (*4M*)

(c) Identify the economic factors which resulted in the construction of the huge Sullom Voe oil terminal in the Shetland Islands. (*4M*)

(d) Comment on both the advantages and disadvantages of the refinery to the Shetland islanders. (*5M*)

(e) If major oil deposits were located in the English Channel, why would exploration and development be in some ways more difficult and for other reasons easier than in the North Sea? (*4M*)

(f) Briefly examine the factors which would encourage and discourage further oil exploration offshore. (*5M*)

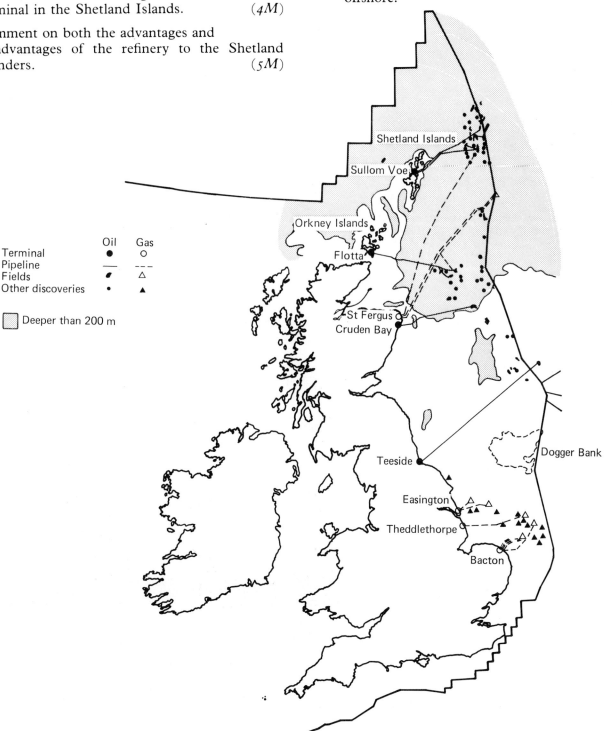

85

(a) What was the percentage increase in world energy demand from 1965 to 1980? What is the estimated percentage increase from 1980 to 2000? (4M)

(b) Figure A shows the highest estimated percentage increase in energy demand 1980–2000 for 'other' regions. Explain. (6M)

(c) Suggest reasons for the two short periods of exceptionally slow growth shown in Figs A and B. (3M)

(d) Why is the relative contribution of oil to world energy supply projected to decline so much in the next two decades? (5M)

(e) In 1980 the contribution of 'Hydro and Other' to world energy supply was 6%. What 'other' sources added to supply in 1980 and which 'other' sources are likely to augment energy supply in the 1980's and 1990's? (7M)

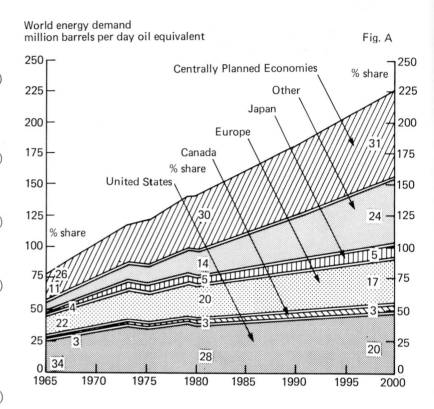

World energy demand
million barrels per day oil equivalent — Fig. A

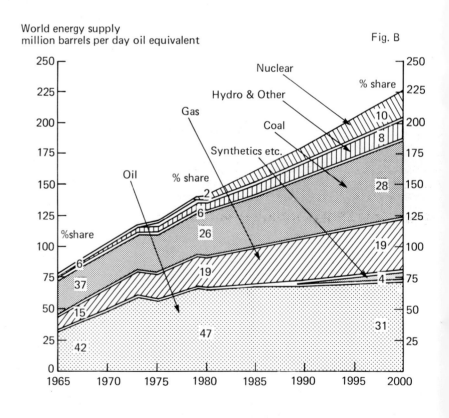

World energy supply
million barrels per day oil equivalent — Fig. B

86

(a) Describe a sampling technique which might yield such results as in the table below. *(6M)*

(b) From the information given, assess the effect of physical factors on land use. *(6M)*

(c) State with reasons the physical regions which are likely to have the highest and lowest population densities. *(5M)*

(d) Describe a statistical technique which would suitably test whether land use varied significantly across the four major geological strata. *(8M)*

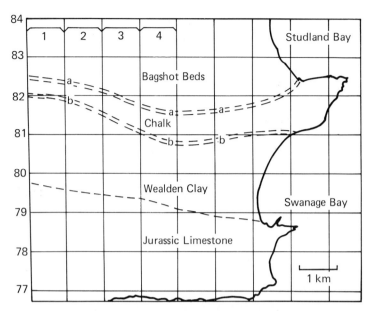

Geology of the Isle of Purbeck. (a) Reading Beds and London Clay (b) Greensand and Gault Clay. Eastings extend from 97 to 06. Numbers 1, 2, 3 and 4 refer to the four study groups

Frequencies of land use related to outcrop

Strata	Observed frequencies of land use				
	(a) Arable	(b) Pastoral	(c) Rough grazing	(d) Woodland wasteland	Total
A Bagshot Beds	9	5	15	18	47
B Chalk	5	3	8	7	23
C Wealden Clay	12	17	3	6	38
D Jurassic Limestone	14	25	15	15	69
Total	40	50	41	46	177

Transect across the Isle of Purbeck

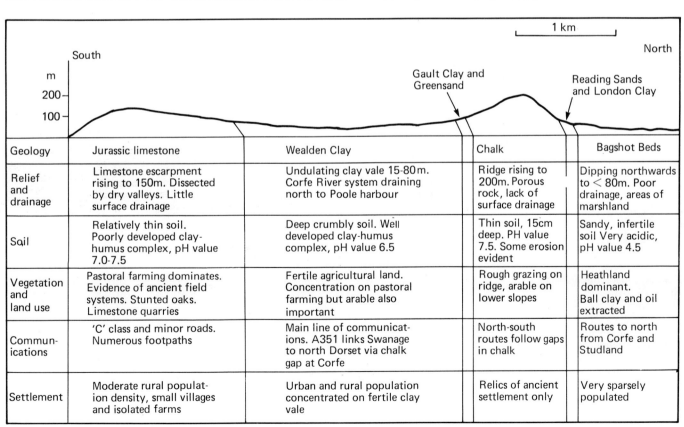

Geology	Jurassic limestone	Wealden Clay	Chalk	Bagshot Beds
Relief and drainage	Limestone escarpment rising to 150m. Dissected by dry valleys. Little surface drainage	Undulating clay vale 15-80m. Corfe River system draining north to Poole harbour	Ridge rising to 200m. Porous rock, lack of surface drainage	Dipping northwards to < 80m. Poor drainage, areas of marshland
Soil	Relatively thin soil. Poorly developed clay-humus complex, pH value 7.0-7.5	Deep crumbly soil. Well developed clay-humus complex, pH value 6.5	Thin soil, 15cm deep. PH value 7.5. Some erosion evident	Sandy, infertile soil Very acidic, pH value 4.5
Vegetation and land use	Pastoral farming dominates. Evidence of ancient field systems. Stunted oaks. Limestone quarries	Fertile agricultural land. Concentration on pastoral farming but arable also important	Rough grazing on ridge, arable on lower slopes	Heathland dominant. Ball clay and oil extracted
Commun-ications	'C' class and minor roads. Numerous footpaths	Main line of communicat-ions. A351 links Swanage to north Dorset via chalk gap at Corfe	North-south routes follow gaps in chalk	Routes to north from Corfe and Studland
Settlement	Moderate rural populat-ion density, small villages and isolated farms	Urban and rural population concentrated on fertile clay vale	Relics of ancient settlement only	Very sparsely populated

87

(a) Define G.D.P. (2M)

(b) What is the extent of the relationship between G.D.P, unemployment and net migration? (7M)

(c) To what extent can economic core and peripheral areas be identified from the information given in the table? (8M)

(d) What are the industrial characteristics usually associated with areas of persistently high unemployment? (4M)

(e) Suggest measures that a government can initiate to redress regional inequalities. (4M)

Region	G.D.P. per capita 1979 (£)	%Unemployment July 1979	Net migration 78/79 (000's)
South East	3251	3.8	−7.7
East Midlands	2824	4.9	10.4
Scotland	2767	8.3	−14.6
West Midlands	2763	6.1	−9.2
North West	2748	7.6	−17.7
Yorkshire and Humberside	2733	6.1	−4.0
East Anglia	2695	4.4	18.3
North	2666	9.2	−10.1
South West	2625	5.7	29.2
Wales	2574	8.3	5.5

88

(a) Explain the wide divergence illustrated by the table between North America/Oceania and the rest of the developed world. (5M)

(b) Why has the total area of agricultural land decreased in the developed regions while it has increased in the developing regions? (5M)

(c) List four possible methods which have helped to improve agricultural output per worker in the developed world. (4M)

(d) What problems can improved agricultural productivity cause in some regions of the developing world? (5M)

(e) Compare the methods employed for one specific type of agriculture between a country in the developed world and a country in the developing world. (6M)

Agricultural land area and corresponding land/worker ratios, world and main regions, 1970 and 1976

	Agricultural land* (millions of hectares)		Agricultural land worker ratio†		Agricultural land/ agricultural population ratio		Agricultural output per agricultural worker		
	1970	1976	1970	1976	1970	1976	1964–1966	1969–1971	1974–1976
World	1459.8	1488.0	1.90	1.88	0.79	0.77	0.46	0.51	0.55
Developed regions	677.9	672.7	7.57	8.79	3.52	7.57	1.94	2.64	3.30
Developed market economies	398.4	394.1	9.92	11.77	4.28	5.11	2.93	3.96	5.00
North America	234.0	232.0	59.97	74.83	25.23	32.96	14.33	19.52	25.72
Western Europe	99.9	96.1	4.42	5.09	1.80	2.10	2.02	2.82	3.56
Oceania	44.3	46.0	79.40	89.88	32.97	37.72	14.14	16.49	19.28
Other developed market economies	20.1	20.0	1.54	1.82	0.74	0.86	0.54	0.74	0.96
Eastern Europe and U.S.S.R.	279.5	278.5	5.66	6.48	3.32	6.48	1.12	1.56	1.96
Developing regions	781.8	815.3	1.15	1.14	0.48	0.46	0.21	0.23	0.25
Developing market economies	645.2	674.1	1.57	1.53	0.60	0.57	0.23	0.25	0.26
Africa	176.5	182.0	2.04	1.96	0.85	0.79	0.18	0.18	0.19
Latin America	133.0	143.6	3.71	3.79	1.16	1.18	0.67	0.75	0.82
Western Asia	78.5	81.1	2.42	2.36	0.81	0.77	0.35	0.38	0.44
Asia and the Pacific	256.1	266.3	1.01	0.98	0.39	0.37	0.16	0.18	0.19
Other developing market economies	1.1	1.1	0.79	0.73	0.37	0.34	0.42	0.42	0.44
Asian centrally planned economies	136.6	141.3	0.51	0.52	0.24	0.24	0.16	0.20	0.22

*Arable land and land under permanent crops.
†Ratio of land area to agricultural labour force.

Output estimates are based on wheat price equivalents.

89

(a) What total percentage do the five products itemised in Table 2 form of (i) total primary products exports and (ii) total exports? (*3M*)

(b) The five products fall into two distinct primary Industries. Name two other primary Industries and a country for each in the less developed world where each is of major economic importance. (*4M*)

(c) What export advantages does Brazil have over the majority of less developed countries? (*6M*)

(d) Like most less developed countries Brazil claims that the terms of world trade are set in favour of the more developed world. Explain. (*6M*)

(e) Import substitution is an important part of Brazil's economic strategy. Explain. (*6M*)

Table 1 Brazilian imports 1978 (U.S. $ millions)

Live animals and vegetable products	1278.0
Wheat	541.2
Other	726.8
Food industry products; alcoholic liquids and vinegar, beverages, tobacco, fats and oils	98.2
Mineral products	4692.7
Petroleum (crude oil)	4093.0
Other	599.7
Products of the chemical and related industries; natural and synthetic rubber and goods manufactured therefrom	2109.3
Textile materials and goods manufactured therefrom	86.3
Common metals and goods manufactured therefrom	964.9
Machines and apparatus, electric and transport equipment	3521.9
Other	887.8
General total	13639.1

Table 2 Brazilian exports 1978 principal primary products (U.S. $ millions)

Coffee	1939.8
Soya beans	1218.7
Grain	169.7
Bran and cake	1049.0
Cocoa	453.8
Raw sugar	195.9
Iron ore	1027.3
Total	4835.7
Primary products	5969.6
Total exports	12650.6

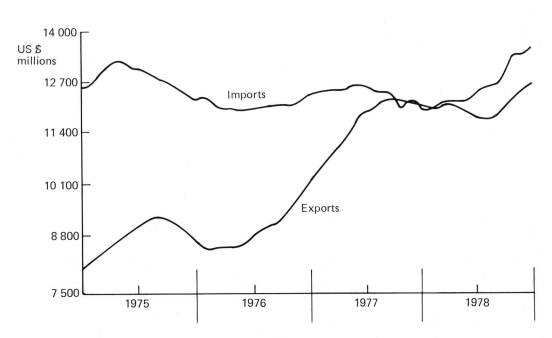

Brazilian trade balance

90

(a) With which regions did the U.K. have a trade surplus in 1980? *(2M)*

(b) Describe how membership of the E.E.C. has affected the destination of exports and the origin of imports for the U.K. *(4M)*

(c) What are the potential economic advantages of membership of a trade association such as the E.E.C? *(7M)*

(d) Name the six original members of the E.E.C. *(2M)*

(e) Identify some of the disputes that have arisen between the member countries of one trade association. *(6M)*

(f) Name two other trade blocs/associations (apart from the E.E.C.), one in the developed world and one in the developing world. Also name two members of each association. *(4M)*

United Kingdom Trade Statistics (£ million. BOP basis seasonally adjusted)

Year	European Community (Inc. Greece)				Rest of W. Europe				North America			
	Exports	Imports	Visible balance	Relative % value	Exports	Imports	Visible balance	Relative % value	Exports	Imports	Visible balance	Relative % value
1964	1266	1228	+38	103	695	611	+84	114	606	1011	−405	60
1965	1300	1277	+23	102	755	629	+126	120	723	1047	−324	69
1966	1397	1411	−14	99	821	651	+170	126	868	1095	−227	79
1967	1405	1624	−219	87	823	754	+69	109	841	1203	−362	70
1968	1752	1980	−228	88	932	988	−56	94	1122	1423	−301	79
1969	2069	2108	−39	98	1111	1049	+62	106	1178	1386	−208	85
1970	2416	2325	+91	104	1330	1295	+35	103	1226	1706	−480	72
1971	2536	2720	−184	93	1450	1470	−20	99	1422	1585	−163	90
1972	2849	3441	−592	83	1551	1733	−182	89	1559	1633	−74	95
1973	3851	5178	−1327	74	1951	2462	−511	79	1879	2153	−274	87
1974	5546	7680	−2134	72	2623	3219	−596	81	2278	2964	−686	77
1975	6227	8734	−2507	71	2972	3240	−268	92	2316	2955	−639	78
1976	8936	11194	−2258	80	3862	4146	−284	93	3065	3887	−822	79
1977	11674	13606	−1932	86	4615	4795	−180	96	3773	4585	−812	82
1978	13348	15863	−2515	84	4385	5224	−839	84	4219	4953	−734	85
1979	17306	19935	−2629	87	5661	6908	−1247	82	4786	5853	−1067	82
1980	20422	19713	+709	104	6838	6907	−69	99	5285	6946	−1661	76

Year	Other Developed Countries				Oil Exporting Countries				Rest of World			
	Exports	Imports	Visible balance	Relative % value	Exports	Imports	Visible balance	Relative % value	Exports	Imports	Visible balance	Relative % value
1964	683	648	+35	105	254	471	−217	54	1064	1142	−78	93
1965	738	619	+119	119	277	459	−182	60	1120	1142	−22	98
1966	714	602	+112	119	297	446	−149	67	1179	1179	−	100
1967	719	632	+87	114	270	430	−160	63	1183	1197	−14	99
1968	806	758	+48	106	364	584	−220	62	1457	1412	+45	103
1969	873	819	+54	107	452	603	−151	75	1586	1513	+73	105
1970	981	822	+159	119	477	597	−120	80	1720	1439	+281	120
1971	1085	851	+234	127	584	802	−218	73	1966	1425	+541	138
1972	940	1083	−143	87	641	775	−134	83	1897	1520	+377	125
1973	1209	1410	−201	86	794	1122	−328	71	2253	2198	+55	103
1974	1719	1615	+104	106	1225	3393	−2168	36	3003	2874	+129	104
1975	1835	1852	−17	99	2275	2948	−673	77	3705	2934	+771	126
1976	1932	2040	−108	95	3172	3854	−682	82	4224	3999	+225	106
1977	2075	2627	−552	79	4335	3421	+914	127	5256	4978	+278	106
1978	2302	2714	−412	85	4680	3033	+1647	154	6129	4818	+1311	127
1979	2485	2771	−286	90	3667	2963	+704	124	6773	5706	+1067	119
1980	2657	2896	−239	92	4822	3980	+842	121	7365	5769	+1596	128